Revitalization is a much needed endeavor in tens of thousands of churches across the United States, but, as Brian Croft writes, both the purist and pragmatist approaches are not enough to sustain true revitalization—a biblical approach is needed. In his book, Croft outlines a simple, biblical guide for church revitalization that can benefit pastors in churches of any size, and lessons from his personal journey augment a thoroughly biblical approach to the task of church revitalization.

THOM S. RAINER
President of LifeWay Christian Resources
Author of *Autopsy of a Deceased Church*

If you only read one book on reclaiming dying churches, read this one. This is certain to become the definitive resource for rescuing dying churches in our generation. Brian brings a rich wealth of personal ministry experience to this book. But more importantly he brings a solid Biblical basis for the activity of rescuing these at risk churches. My heart was warmed, my spirit encouraged and my boldness to replant dying churches was strengthened with every page I read. I commend this book to you. Read it and read it again.

MARK CLIFTON
Senior Director, Replant
North American Mission Board

Some books are written from ivory towers. *Biblical Church Revitalization* is not one of them. Brian Croft writes about church revitalization as one who has labored in the trenches of this work for several years. Croft sets forth both the challenges and joys of this kingdom work. Biblical, practical, filled with pastoral wisdom – this book is a "must read" on the topic of revitalizing churches.

TIMOTHY K. BEOUGHER
Associate Dean, Billy Graham School of Missions, Evangelism and Ministry,
Billy Graham Professor of Evangelism and Church Growth,
The Southern Baptist Theological Seminary, Louisville, Kentucky

I loved this book. Immensely practical and completely realistic. This should be a must read for all pastors and church planters when it comes to handling expectations of the minist

Senior Pastor, Niddrie Commu
Founder

I rejoice in the appearance of this book by Brian Croft. He discards unhelpful popular approaches to church revitalization and instead advocates church health rather than church growth! This may be achieved, he argues, by God's Spirit working through God's word bringing true spiritual life to a local church. The book is both biblical and balanced, practical and personal as Croft weaves together a rich blend of biblical exegesis and pastoral wisdom forged over many years of experience at the coal-face of ministry. Here are sound principles which are thoroughly transferrable across time and culture. The book is a "must-read" for theological students, pastors in service and anyone who is burdened about dying and divided churches.

EDWIN EWART
Principal, The Irish Baptist College, Belfast

This book is a gift to pastors and church leaders who are yearning to see God do a work of spiritual transformation in a dying church. Brian Croft writes from a refreshingly clear and humble faith in the sufficiency of God's Spirit and God's word to bring about this transformation. Read it prayerfully and humbly, put its precepts into practice, and see God do what He alone can do – give life to the dead!

ANDREW DAVIS
Senior Pastor, First Baptist Church of Durham, North Carolina
Author, *An Infinite Journey*

Churches are dying a sad, slow death across the landscape of Baptist life and hundreds stand in need of new life in much the same way as Ezekiel's valley of dry bones. Can these dry bones live? By God's grace, the answer is a resounding yes, and Brian Croft takes you along on a compelling journey that saw the Lord take a dead church and breathe new life into it by means of a faithful, biblical ministry. This book is not your average, dry-as-dust "how to" volume that offers a few principles that promise to serve as a silver bullet for a dying congregation, but offers true, biblical meat that, rightly applied, will serve to build the church of Jesus Christ. And, it tells a riveting story in which God brought back one congregation from the dead. Brian is the quintessential pastor to write this book for such a time as ours.

JEFF ROBINSON
Pastor, Christ Fellowship Church of Louisville, Kentucky
Senior Editor, The Gospel Coalition.

FOREWORD BY HARRY L. REEDER

BIBLICAL CHURCH REVITALIZATION
SOLUTIONS FOR DYING & DIVIDED CHURCHES

BRIAN CROFT

CHRISTIAN
FOCUS

Copyright © Brian Croft 2016

paperback ISBN 978-1-78191-766-4
epub ISBN 978-1-78191-859-3
mobi ISBN 978-1-78191-860-9

10 9 8 7 6 5 4 3 2 1

Published in 2016
by
Christian Focus Publications Ltd,
Geanies House, Fearn, Ross-shire,
IV20 1TW, Great Britain.

www.christianfocus.com

Cover design by moose77.com

Printed by Bell & Bain, Glasgow

Contents

Dedication

To my wife, Cara:

Knowing you were always with me and
for me in this difficult work made all the difference.

Foreword

Brian Croft has done us a great service. How? He has thoughtfully and I am sure prayerfully produced an inspirational, instructive and insightful volume on how to minister effectively to churches that are dying, stagnant or declining—specifically how to implement a ministry of church revitalization that is not only biblical but is also solution oriented. So at Brian's invitation here are a few paragraphs designed to encourage you as to how important and valuable the contents which fill every page of this book are. Furthermore this book read with a teachable spirit has the potential to become a life-changing and ministry-renovating encounter.

The statistics concerning the status of the Christian church in North America are not encouraging. In fact they are starkly discouraging. Why? Because an honest appraisal reveals that the church in North America is in a sustained statistical free fall. There are multiple evidences. Let me share two of them. The first statistical evidence is the unmistakable fact that the number of local churches in North America is diminishing. To be specific, if you take the number of churches in existence at the beginning of the year, add the number of churches that were planted throughout the year and then subtract the number of churches that closed that year, the result is an astonishing net loss of churches. Specifically there has been an average net loss of 3,500 churches each year over the last twenty-plus years. The second statistic is that of the remaining churches, 88 to 91 per cent of them are dying.

At the moment our strategic response to this phenomenon is the call to plant more churches. While church planting is essential to the strategy of fulfilling the Great Commission as evidenced in the New Testament, the strategy isn't working today. Why? Let me suggest it isn't working because there is another strategy revealed in the New Testament and employed by the Apostles that is being neglected. That strategy is an intentional commitment to church revitalization which, if employed, would result in fewer churches closing. The plain fact is that the Bible not only affirms church planting, it also affirms church revitalization. So here are three biblical church revitalization principles to initiate your journey through this book, which intentionally and effectively promotes the strategy of church revitalization.

1) The objective is church health not church growth

Whether it is church planting or church revitalization, the objective is not statistical growth. The objective is church health. Certainly statistical growth is a desired consequence—more churches, more conversions, more disciple-makers, etc. But our ministry objective in church planting or church revitalization is not to be 'big' nor is it to be 'small'. We must dismiss both the notion that 'big defines success' or that 'small defines faithful'. Why? Success is not the verdict if a church is 'five miles wide and one inch deep' nor is faithfulness assured in a church that is 'one inch wide and five miles deep'. A better idea and more importantly a biblical objective would be a church 'body' that is spiritually healthy and increasingly marked as both 'deep and wide'.

2) Statistical growth is not the objective of church revitalization but it is an expected consequence

> *And the word of God continued to increase, and the number of the disciples multiplied greatly in Jerusalem, and a great many of the priests became obedient to the faith.* (Acts 6:7 ESV)

In Acts 6:7 spiritual vitality is described as the *'Word of the Lord grew'*. Spiritual vitality then produces functional growth in the life of the church evidenced by prayer, worship, evangelism, disciple-making, etc. Functional growth normally leads to statistical growth – *'the numbers increased'*. So then what is the objective? The objective of church revitalization is simply yet profoundly a God-glorifying, Christ-centered, Holy-Spirit empowered, Gospel-driven and Bible-shaped church expanding, not by church growth techniques but, by an intentional commitment to a Gospel disciple-making ministry as profiled in the church of Jerusalem in Acts 2:42-47 (ESV):

> *And they devoted themselves to the apostles' teaching and the fellowship, to the breaking of bread and the prayers. And awe came upon every soul, and many wonders and signs were being done through the apostles. And all who believed were together and had all things in common. And they were selling their possessions and belongings and distributing the proceeds to all, as any had need. And day by day, attending the temple together and breaking bread in their homes they received their food with glad and generous hearts, praising God and having favor with all the people. And the Lord added to their number day by day those who were being saved.*

3) Church revitalization is not simply a desirable strategy but when united to church planting it is the apostolic model to 'turn the world upside down' for the glory of God

There are thirteen words recorded in Acts 17:6 (ESV) that I would love to hear one more time. A pagan opponent of the Gospel from the continent of Europe (less than twenty-five years after the ascension of Jesus) uttered them as an invective of abject frustration— 'these people who have turned the world upside down have come here also.'

We know 'who' *turned the world upside down*—the Holy Spirit through the body of Christ. We know 'what' *turned the world upside down*—the power of the Gospel. But what ought to also capture our attention as we examine the expansion of the Kingdom from Jerusalem to Judea and Samaria and to the world is 'how' they *turned the world upside down*. The answer to that question is unmistakable if we examine the documented ministry of the Apostle Paul and his team as they went city to city in the first missionary trip gloriously revealed in the book of Acts.

The Acts 13–15 record of the first missionary trip reveals a repeated ministry formula. As the Apostolic team entered the city they would engage in Gospel evangelism and disciple-making. Next they would plant a Gospel church in the city. Then they would respond to prevailing needs in the city with Gospel deeds of love and mercy. Finally they would ensure the well-being of the new church by appointing Gospel leaders. If that was not possible they would leave a portion of the team behind until indigenous leaders could be installed, since the health and vitality of a local church is directly related to the health and vitality of its leadership. After the first General Assembly of the burgeoning New Testament church the Apostle Paul in conversation with his mentor and friend Barnabas outlined his proposed agenda for a second missionary journey in Acts 15 and 16. Interestingly the agenda for the second missionary journey was the same as the first missionary journey except for one significant addition—church revitalization:

> *Let's return and visit the brothers in every city where we proclaimed the Word of the Lord and see how they are ... He went through Syria and Cilicia 'strengthening' the churches ... So the churches were strengthened in the faith and they increased in numbers daily* (ESV).

The result of the second missionary journey is summed up in Acts 17 (ESV) as 'turning the world upside down'. This was the result of God's Providence leading the Apostolic team to do on the second missionary journey what they did on the first missionary journey— Gospel evangelism and disciple-making; Gospel church planting; Gospel deeds of love and mercy and developing Gospel leaders, except for one additive. On the second journey they introduced Gospel church revitalization as they 'strengthened the churches' planted on the first missionary journey.

In a word, by embracing the world-shaking Apostolic model local churches and denominations would not only have an intentional commitment to planting Gospel-healthy churches but will also be intentionally committed to the ministry of revitalizing churches. That would result in an increased number of church plants because, not only would we be closing fewer churches, we would now have more Gospel-healthy mother churches producing Gospel-healthy daughter churches instead of today's church planting, which in many cases is simply subdividing unhealthy churches. Enjoy the content in this book but even more importantly employ the content of this book and by God's grace we could once again hear ... 'these men who have turned the world upside down have come here also' (Acts 17:6 ESV).

For Christ, the Gospel and His Church

Harry L. Reeder III
Senior Pastor, Briarwood Presbyterian Church, Birmingham, Alabama

Author of
From Embers to a Flame: How God can revitalize your church

Acknowledgements

Brian would like to thank:

- Christian Focus Publications for believing in this book and the needed work of church revitalization around the world.

- Harry Reeder for his willingness to write the Foreword as well as his example in waving the banner to help struggling churches find new life.

- The Southern Baptist Theological Seminary, The Mathena Family, Jim Stitzinger, Eric Bancroft, Tim Beougher, Dan McGill, and all others who have made it a great joy to serve in the Mathena Center for Church Revitalization. I am grateful for your partnership in this work.

- The first class of Mathena Center interns: Henry, Sean, Cody, Charlie, Randall, and Michael. Our stimulating discussions and your eager teachability helped clarify and solidify much of the material found in this book.

- For all those who read this book in its earlier stages and gave invaluable feedback. Each of you made this book stronger, clearer, and better.

- Mike and Dana Ferguson whose faithful service and friendship were essential to our survival in those first few years. No one but God knows the depth and value of the role you played in that crucial season.

- Scott Wells whose gifts to write and edit have made many of my books immensely stronger and clearer. It is a great joy to serve alongside you in Practical Shepherding.

- My church, Auburndale Baptist Church, who remain the sweetest testimony to me that God can breathe life into struggling churches. Our church is a special place because of you and the Lord's work in you.

- My wife, Cara and our children who know better than anyone of the difficulties that accompany this work. You were a healing balm to me throughout the years of chaos, and continue to be for my weary soul.

- The Chief Shepherd, Jesus, for the gift of knowing You, being loved by You, and the privilege of serving as an undershepherd of Your people until You return.

Introduction

The numbers are staggering. Experts estimate that approximately 1,000 local churches close their doors every year. What is even more disheartening about this statistic is that number only reflects churches with the Southern Baptist Convention (SBC)—my denomination.[1] Imagine how that number grows if you added the number of closing local churches from other established denominations, which some assert are between 3,500 and 4,000 churches annually.[2] Needless to say, we have an epidemic on our hands. Although God continues in part to build His church through church planting, churches are not being planted and lasting near the rate of those that permanently shut their doors each year.

It is good and right to be burdened by the reality of the extinguishing of once thriving local churches that previously were gospel lights in their communities. Pastors are quitting. Beautiful,

---

1. R. Albert Mohler Jr. (ed.), *Guide To Church Revitalization*. (Louisville: SBTS Press 2015), p. 13.

2. Ed Stetzer and Mike Dodson, *Comeback Churches: How 300 Churches Turned Around and Yours Can Too* (Nashville: B&H 2007), p. 19.

historic church buildings are being auctioned to the highest bidder. No doubt the burden that many who love Christ's bride feel, is a burden we too should feel. The weight of this burden has resulted in an unprecedented movement to do something about these dying churches. Emerging in a variety of denominations, it has been labeled, 'Church Revitalization' and/or 'Church Replanting'.

Having engaged in my own pastoral work of church revitalization prior to the inception of this movement and having observed this movement during that time, I have noticed two commonly unhelpful approaches to this undertaking: the *Pragmatist* and the *Purist*.

The Pragmatist

The pragmatist seeks to revive and grow a dying church through clever gimmicks and appealing programs that work to bring about specific, desired results. These results usually are numerically based, driven by robust evangelistic efforts that rely heavily on man's abilities and gifts. Although the Bible and God's Spirit are often given verbal acknowledgement and have a place in the mix, the desired physical and numeric results become the chief end and driving purpose of the work and the power of revitalization ultimately is found in the cleverness of man. Consequently, results and broad appeal become more important than faithfulness to a specific design God may have for His church that might not produce the same numeric results. To the pragmatist, the desired numeric result becomes the end that justifies embracing whatever means are necessary to accomplish it.

The Purist

The purist approaches the task of church revitalization from a strict adherence to biblical principles based on the centrality of God's word. This frequently manifests itself in ways such as an extremely narrow view of biblical forms of worship. While we all must strive for a biblical approach, there is also a very subtle danger lurking in the background of this approach that can become a major pitfall, and it hides in the heart motives of the revitalizing pastor. If not careful, the pastor's convictions can almost imperceptibly shift from being a conviction about the centrality of God's word to become a conviction not to be like the pragmatist. Consequently, the purist celebrates being anti-appeal and anti-creative, and pridefully shuns anything that might appear as entertainment, or consumeristic and worldly. The purist perceives himself as firmly standing on the promises of the power of the word of God to breathe revitalizing life into a congregation. But in reality he is merely squatting on a rigid legalism, intentionally making the church somewhat unappealing in order to discern who indeed is committed to God, His word, His people, and His church.

A Biblical Approach

There is a balanced, biblical approach to the work of revitalization that is both more effective as well as more faithful to God's design for the local church. This method rests its full weight on the truth that God's spirit working through His word is the only way to bring true lasting spiritual life to a local church. And yet it also values the truth that it is good and right for the bride of Christ to look beautiful and appealing to God's people and even to intrigue those who are hostile to Christ in the world. This approach incorporates both the deep conviction that God's power by His Spirit and word does the work and the fact that God also uses creativity, passion, unique gifts, and the zeal of His leaders and people to breathe life and build His church.

This biblical approach advocates that the local church *should* be appealing, but for specific scriptural reasons: passionate biblical preaching, loving sacrificial fellowship, practical gospel application, zealous soul care, intentional evangelism, and authentic Christ-likeness—to name a few. This method's goal is to see new life and growth come to a local church, but not at the expense of a faithful pursuit of God's design for the local church. Church health according to God's biblical design becomes the ultimate goal, not numbers. God's power is found in Him building His church the way He wants to build His church; it is not defined by any worldly success.

It is this more biblical approach that I wish to advocate in this book. The details of this method are described in three main sections: Church Revitalization being Defined, Diagnosed, and Done:

- *Defined:* This section explains this approach, highlighting why God's word through His Spirit is not only the power of God that brings revitalization, but is also our detailed

17

guidebook to know how best to approach this difficult yet noble task as a pastor.

- *Diagnosed:* This section highlights five key biblical areas that consistently mark the core issues of most churches that need to be addressed to experience new life. All five areas are identified and evaluated, then viewed through a biblical lens to help a pastor know how to identify the dysfunction in these areas in his own church and consider biblical solutions.

- *Done:* This section shares the narrative of my ten year revitalization journey at my current church and the hard, painful lessons I learned in the process. This is meant to be a moving, redemptive story of God's power and grace in me and my church that happened as a result of applying the biblical approach that is advocated in this book.

My deep conviction for this method comes from engaging in this work of church revitalization for many years in several areas. First, working as a pastor for over twenty years. The church, of which I went to be the Senior Pastor in 2003, had experienced over three decades of conflict and decline and was approximately two to three years from closing its doors if nothing changed. All the gimmicks and clever methods had been tried and had failed. I knew I was not gifted enough to salvage this church in my own power. Only God could breathe life into something so far gone. By His sovereign grace, I watched Him do it.

Second, laboring as a trainer and mentor of pastors and aspiring ones. The most gifted and clever pastor is still too sinful, broken and weak to save a church under his own power. Men gifted for pastoral ministry need to be trained in a specific, unique way to be able to persevere in this difficult, unique, and noble work. This book is how I train and prepare men for this unique ministry who are in my local church, involved with Practical Shepherding[3], as well as in the seminary where I serve.

---

3. Practical Shepherding is an international non-profit ministry to serve pastors and church leaders who are laboring in the trenches of pastoral ministry. You can learn more about this ministry at www.practicalshepherding.com.

Third, serving as a consultant to hurting, dying churches. The methodology advocated in this book comes as a result of the undeniably consistent patterns of dysfunction in most every church I work with and what each church must experience to gain new life. God's design works and is the only way a dying, struggling church can experience lasting spiritual life.

Finally, passion for the gospel and Christ's church. It is the gospel that is the power of God unto salvation (Rom. 1:16). It is a stunning testimony of the power of God and the gospel when a healthy, vibrant local church with a spiritual life that is so present in God's people draws other followers of Jesus, and a hostile world looks with curiosity and wonder.

There is a unique and special power and testimony in not just a vibrant local church full of life, but an old historic one that had lost its way, was on life support, and into which God saw fit to breathe life once again. What better testimony that God is a God who raises the dead than watching it happen to dead churches all around the world? But make no mistake. God is the one who must do it. Only God's power is sufficient to accomplish it. Read this book and consider this biblical approach. Consider as the Holy Spirit balances God's mighty power at work in faithful, persistent, yet broken jars of clay to build His church and make Christ gloriously known.

Section I:
Church Revitalization – Defined

Chapter 1

POWER

How does God revitalize a dying church?

WITHIN one specific decade I performed well over a hundred funerals. I have seen a lot of different, gut-wrenching ways that people process and grieve the loss of a loved one, but the actions of one particular woman who had lost her spouse sticks out in my mind. She fell on the casket and started shaking her deceased husband trying to get him to wake up, a living picture that captured the limitations of our humanity. As God's image bearers we have the potential to accomplish great things, but something even the strongest man in the world can never do is wake up a dead person. There are some things that are impossible for us as human beings to do in this life. But nothing is impossible with God. God's power is so great, He can do anything. God can even raise the dead. The prophet Ezekiel reminds us of this great truth by revealing what only God in His great power can do. Arguably there is no clearer demonstration of God's life-giving power than in Ezekiel 37.

The preceding chapter, Ezekiel 36, vividly describes one of the greatest promises in the Old Testament, the New Covenant. God promised His rebellious and hurting people, who were in exile, that a day would come when God would make a New Covenant with them that would transform them from the inside out. Among the benefits God promised in this covenant were:

- The indwelling of God's Spirit
- Cleansing from impurity
- A new heart

As wonderful as this New Covenant promise is in Ezekiel 36, one can be left with a nagging question by the end of the chapter—how would God accomplish this? God had made a promise, but how could Israel know if God can and would deliver on this promise? How could they know God had the power and means to do what He said He would do?

This is why Ezekiel 37 is so important. The valley of dry bones is one of the most well-known images in all of Scripture, but it is its context and placement that makes it especially powerful to read as it explains how God says He will do what He promised. It shows that God has the power to do the impossible—even raise the dead. Dying churches are no exception.

This chapter seeks to demonstrate the power of God vividly displayed in this vision of the valley of dry bones. It is an exposition of Ezekiel 37 that seeks to answer this question, How does God revitalize a dying and divided church? And here's the answer:

> A church is revitalized by the power of God through the Spirit of God at work through the word of God by means of a faithful shepherd of God.

Ezekiel 37 reveals that God is powerful enough to do what a dying and divided church needs: Breathe life where there is no life and unite those who cannot be united.

God breathes life where there is no life

The first half of Ezekiel 37 is a vision that reeks of death and despair and it leaves the sense that this valley is too far gone for any life to exist again.

> The hand of the Lord was upon me, and He brought me out by the Spirit of the Lord and set me down in the middle of the valley; and it was full of bones. ²He caused me to pass among them round about, and behold, there were very many on the surface of the valley; and lo, they were very dry. ³He said to me, 'Son of man, can these bones live?' And I answered, 'O Lord God, You know.' ⁴Again He said to me, 'Prophesy over these bones and say to them, "O dry bones, hear the word of the Lord." ⁵Thus says the Lord God to these bones, "Behold, I will cause breath to enter you that you may come to life. ⁶I will put sinews on you, make flesh grow back on you, cover you with skin and put breath in you that you may come alive; and you will know that I am the Lord".'
>
> ⁷So I prophesied as I was commanded; and as I prophesied, there was a noise, and behold, a rattling; and the bones came together, bone to its bone. ⁸And I looked, and behold, sinews were on them, and flesh grew and skin covered them; but there was no breath in them. ⁹Then He said to me, 'Prophesy to the breath, prophesy, son of man, and say to the breath, "Thus says the Lord God, 'Come from the four winds, O breath, and breathe on these slain, that they come to life'".' ¹⁰So I prophesied as He commanded me, and the breath came into them, and they came to life and stood on their feet, an exceedingly great army.
>
> ¹¹Then He said to me, 'Son of man, these bones are the whole house of Israel; behold, they say, "Our bones are dried up and our hope has perished. We are completely cut off." ¹²Therefore prophesy and say to them, "Thus says the Lord God, 'Behold, I will open your graves and cause you to come up out of your graves, My people; and I will bring you into

the land of Israel. [13]Then you will know that I am the Lord, when I have opened your graves and caused you to come up out of your graves, My people. [14]I will put My Spirit within you and you will come to life, and I will place you on your own land. Then you will know that I, the Lord, have spoken and done it,' declares the Lord'" (Ezek. 37:1-14)

God asks Ezekiel a pressing question that drives this whole chapter and vision. God by His Spirit sets Ezekiel down in a valley full of dry bones and asks, 'Son of man, can these bones live?' Since God knows everything, He is not asking because He doesn't know the answer, but to make a point. The point is made in Ezekiel's response, 'O Lord God, you know.'

We can understand Ezekiel's response as not just, 'God, you know …' but an affirmation that only God knows and only God could make these dead, dry bones live. From this question and answer, God proves this dialogue to be true—God is the only one who can breathe life where there is no life. God through His word by His Spirit is the catalyst to bring this life.

God brings life by declaring His word. God commands Ezekiel to prophesy over these bones and declare this word to those bones, 'God said to these bones, "Behold, I will cause breath to enter you that you may come to life".' In the power of God, God spoke all creation into existence when nothing existed. Now in the power of God, He says, I will take these dead, dry bones, put flesh back on them and breathe life into them all that you may know that I am the Lord.

God breathes life by fulfilling His word. The power of God is not simply seen in His declaration, but in the fulfillment of it. God declares His word, but we find that word fulfilled just as He says, 'So I prophesied as I was commanded; and as I prophesied, there was a sound, and behold, a rattling; and the bones came together, bone to its bone' (esv). Verses 8-10 then describe God's promise to breathe life into these dead, dry bones coming to pass as these dry bones become an exceedingly great army.

God breathes life by explaining His word. This vision is spoken to God's people Israel who are in exile, suffering, and living out the consequences of rebellion against God. A pressing question after hearing the promise of the New Covenant could be, So how does this happen? The explanation of this vision in verses 11-14 answers that nagging question. These bones are the whole house of Israel that is dried up and hopeless. This vision is a picture of what God promises to do with His spiritually dead, rebellious people, 'Behold, I will open your graves and cause you to come up out of your graves, My people; and I will bring you into the land of Israel. Then you will know that I am the Lord, when I do this ... I will put My Spirit within you and you will come to life.'

God's people were so far gone that they were without hope. They have as much hope to save themselves and give themselves life as that grieving spouse trying to shake her husband awake at the funeral. According to the book of Ezekiel God's people are in such a place of hopeless despair that only God and His power and might can do what we cannot. What can God even do? In one of the few places in all of the Old Testament we are reminded that God is so powerful that He can even raise the dead. God is so powerful that He can do what is impossible for any of us as humans to ever do—breathe life into that which is dead. The point of this strategically placed chapter in Ezekiel is this: it is with this power that only comes from God that God can fulfill the promise of a new heart, a new spirit that dwells in His people, change them, cleanse them, and bring them back to life (Ezek. 36). The same is true for dying churches.

God unites where there is enmity

There is a second image that covers the second half of Ezekiel 37.

> [15]The word of the Lord came again to me saying, [16]'And you, son of man, take for yourself one stick and write on it, "For Judah and for the sons of Israel, his companions"; then take another stick and write on it, "For Joseph, the stick of Ephraim and all the house of Israel, his companions". [17]Then join them for yourself one to another into one stick, that they may become one in your hand. [18]When the sons of your people speak to you saying, "Will you not declare to us what you mean by these?" [19]say to them, "Thus says

the Lord God, 'Behold, I will take the stick of Joseph, which is in the hand of Ephraim, and the tribes of Israel, his companions; and I will put them with it, with the stick of Judah, and make them one stick, and they will be one in My hand'." [20]The sticks on which you write will be in your hand before their eyes. [21]Say to them, "Thus says the Lord God, 'Behold, I will take the sons of Israel from among the nations where they have gone, and I will gather them from every side and bring them into their own land; [22]and I will make them one nation in the land, on the mountains of Israel; and one king will be king for all of them; and they will no longer be two nations and no longer be divided into two kingdoms. [23]They will no longer defile themselves with their idols, or with their detestable things, or with any of their transgressions; but I will deliver them from all their dwelling places in which they have sinned, and will cleanse them. And they will be My people, and I will be their God.

[24]'My servant David will be king over them, and they will all have one shepherd; and they will walk in My ordinances and keep My statutes and observe them. [25]They will live on the land that I gave to Jacob My servant, in which your fathers lived; and they will live on it, they, and their sons and their sons' sons, forever; and David My servant will be their prince forever. [26]I will make a covenant of peace with them; it will be an everlasting covenant with them. And I will place them and multiply them, and will set My sanctuary in their midst forever. [27]My dwelling place also will be with them; and I will be their God, and they will be My people. [28]And the nations will know that I am the Lord who sanctifies Israel, when My sanctuary is in their midst forever"'.'

This next vision is about Ezekiel taking one stick that represents Judah and another stick that represents Israel and combining them to be one stick. God explains this prophetic drama as the unification of the two divided kingdoms of Israel and Judah. After the reign of King Solomon, civil war resulted in the nation of Israel splitting into two kingdoms. Later both these kingdoms would be scattered even more because of the exile. God shows that His power is able not just to breathe life into that which is dead, but to unite that which could not be united.

God unites the two estranged nations by gathering them. He promises, 'I will gather them from every side and bring them into their own land; and I will make them one nation in the land.' God scattered and divided them in judgment, but in the New Covenant He promises to unite them as one people where He will be their God and they will be His people.

God unites by cleansing them. God promises to change them in such a way that they will no longer defile themselves with their idols or transgressions. He promises to deliver them from all their dwelling places where they sinned and cleanse them. There can be all kinds of things that divide a people, but if there would be one thing that would unite God's rebellious people, it would be forgiveness. God's forgiveness can reconcile and unite sinners at enmity against one another. God's promise of cleansing would unite them as God's redeemed people.

God unites through one king. This one king already referenced as 'My servant David' is the Messiah. God promises He alone will be king over this unified people. They will have one shepherd and He will lead them to keep God's commands. One king will be over them and 'they will no longer be two nations, but one'.

God unites through His presence. God says, 'They will live on the land that I gave to Jacob my servant, in which your fathers lived.' This is the Promised Land that points back to God's covenant with Abraham about this one nation before it even existed. Now, God in His great power under the New Covenant will bring these fractured and divided kingdoms into one nation again. God will make a covenant of peace with them and it will be an everlasting covenant in which He declares, 'My dwelling place also will be with them; and I will be their God, and they will be My people.'

God does all this to dwell among His people and to declare to the nations that they may know that I am the Lord who sanctifies Israel. This is quite the redemption. God's people are far from Him, His presence has left (Ezek. 11), they are in exile, their beloved city has been destroyed, and they are scattered in despair among the nations. Now comes this promise of a full reversal: cleansing from sin, a new heart to obey, one king to rule forever over them as one nation, and God's presence to always dwell with His people. God unites His people by His power and cuts through the hostility and hatred that existed among the tribes to make them one nation—one people who belong to God.

Dying, divided local churches

This significant word from God through the prophet Ezekiel clearly has its own context and narrative found in a dark time and history with God's people. It is important to acknowledge that this word from Ezekiel was not spoken with the New Testament church, nor a modern day church revitalization movement in mind. There are, however, principles seen in this passage that are re-affirmed in the New Testament that speak to how God moves in His power to accomplish His sovereign purposes. Just as we see God moving among His people during this dark time of exile with His rebellious people, we too can gain insight into how an unchanging, powerful God still works in His church and people today. That is, God is always working to fulfill His promises and purposes to breathe life into His people and unite them where enmity exists.

If there are two primary marks of churches needing revitalization, it would arguably be the absence of spiritual life and the presence of hostile division among those in the church. Either of these realities can single-handedly kill a church over time, but when both are present, death is imminent. The only hope for these kinds of churches is the same hope for Israel in the darkness of their exile—the power of God. God's design is for that power to come by God's Spirit moving through His spoken word. As we see illustrated in the valley of dry bones, that power harnessed by God's Spirit and word can breathe life where there is no life and bring unity where there is division.

The rest of this book seeks to wave the banner that only God and His power can truly revitalize a dying, divided church, and God's design to accomplish this is found through His Spirit at work in His word. Because of this, the Bible, especially the Pauline

Epistles, become the driving force of this book to guide us in the particularities and complexities of this noble work of revitalization. The aim is that you will see not just that God's design of Spirit and word is what breathes life and unites His people in His church, but that God's word speaks to the details, direction, and strategies of how this work is to be approached. Read this book with an eye to learn how biblically to approach this work, but most of all read with a growing faith that God is powerful enough to revitalize the most dead and divided church. As the valley of dry bones teaches us, when He does there is no doubt who brought the life.

CHAPTER 2

PREPARATION
How does a pastor prepare to revitalize a church?

THE unprecedented need to revitalize churches in our modern day brings with it a weighty and timely dilemma—who will go and revitalize? Where are the men that can be sent to pastor these dying churches? Here lies the great task as we look upon the sea of dying churches needing certain men with specific pastoral gifts, an intentional calling, and a resolve to persevere. They must be trained. To some degree, every pastor of a revitalization work needs to be evaluated and trained biblically like any pastor would.

There are detailed qualifications and characteristics that need to be identified in every pastor (1 Tim. 3:1-7; Titus 1:5-9). There are specific imperatives that are necessary for a pastor to understand rightfully his calling and to engage faithfully in the work of pastoral ministry (1 Pet. 5:1-5; Acts 20:28; Heb. 13:17). There are, however, other unique qualities that, although they may not be as clearly identified in Scripture, are essential for a man to know whether pastoring a church needing revitalization is wise for him in particular.

The Church Revitalization team of the North American Mission Board (NAMB) has created a list of eight characteristics that capture well what these other unique and essential qualities are in someone feeling a call to pastor a dying church:

- Visionary shepherd
- High tolerance for pain
- Respect and passion for the church's legacy
- Passion for multi-generational ministry
- A resourceful generalist
- Tactical patience
- Emotional awareness
- Spousal perseverance[1]

These eight qualities highlight well the profile of a man who could flourish in the balanced biblical approach conveyed in this book and avoid the pitfalls of both the Pragmatist and the Purist. Once a man has been biblically assessed and sifted through these eight characteristics, there remain three areas of which a man seeking revitalization work needs to be aware and in which he needs to be trained that also answer three key questions as the revitalizer enters a church: Pastoral Theology, Healthy Ecclesiology, and Personal Soul Care.

What do I do? (Pastoral Theology)

So many of the mistakes and missteps a pastor makes in a church needing revitalization comes from a lack of knowledge of what to do. The absence of clear thinking on this matter causes a pastor to listen to all kinds of different voices and hastily react to what he finds and hears in his church. Some say change everything immediately. Others urge a pastor to look outside the church for new life. If a

---

1. These eight qualities are found both on the NAMB Replanting brochure and are explained more fully in a forthcoming book, Mark Clifton, *Reclaiming Glory: Hope for dying churches.* (Nashville: B & H).

pastor does not have a solid handle on what to do and even a better idea of what not to do, he will react and make quick decisions based on the mess he finds.

A pastor needs to be trained not to be reactionary regarding the dysfunction and turmoil he finds, but to have a clear plan on how his time should be spent during his first few years, regardless of what problems he inherits. The best approach for a pastor when entering a dysfunctional, dying congregation is to simply be a pastor to those people. This is why pastors need to be trained in the practicalities of pastoral theology so to be equipped in the work of the ministry. A simple definition of pastoral theology is the application of biblical theology in a pastoral manner for the purpose of caring for God's people. That is, pastoral theology informs a pastor of the day-to-day tasks of a pastor with the aim of ministering to God's people. These tasks include such things as preaching, praying, visiting the sick, caring for widows, discipling others, raising up leaders, encouraging the weak, conducting weddings and funerals, to name a few.

The key to applying pastoral theology in church revitalization is centered on these two principles: the biblical tasks of a pastor for the sake of caring for the flock. The absence of biblical pastoral theology often leads to pragmatism. The absence of intentional, wise, and creative desires to minister to God's people and meet them where they are can create the purist. A pastor should not place the crushing expectation on himself of transforming the church in eighteen months, but should simply come with a clear vision of what his calling is as a shepherd and pastor and do that with all his might. First and foremost, prepare to just be patient and shepherd the souls of the people who are there when you arrive. This allows a pastor to do what he can do and allows God time to do what only He can do.

Where do we go? (Healthy Ecclesiology)

Unachievable goals can be the death of every pastor's ministry. The best way for a pastor to set himself up for failure is to set a specific number of new church members as the goal for his church needing revitalization. Even if a pastor reaches his numeric goal, that doesn't assure life. All churches need to allow church health, not numbers, to be the gauge of authentic spiritual life and growth. Dwindling numbers in a church may expose a lack of church health that was hidden during a church's numeric heyday. While a pastor does the daily work of a pastor immediately upon his arrival, he needs to be praying and seeking guidance from God for a vision on where to take the church—that is church health.

The first principle in pursuing church health is that the process from which it results is a slow one. The vision of where to go must be clear from the beginning, but the implementation of it must take years. If a man needs to lose one hundred pounds, it doesn't matter how hard he works the first two months, becoming healthy takes time. In my experience, it takes a minimum of five years before a pastor can begin to see real, lasting fruit of his ministry that points to church health. You will later read my story where the first five years of my ministry were treacherous. Had I left at the end of five years (which I almost did) I would have missed most of the fruit God brought from my early labors.

Once there is a resolve to go slow, a pastor needs to realize that every local church is to display God's glory and that is best accomplished through pursuing church health. For a church to move toward lasting health and life, the structure of the church needs to be evaluated in order to determine whether it is conducive to facilitating healthy growth. Variations of church polity can all have versions of church health, but for the purposes of this book I would like to address the typical Southern Baptist Church structure and how church health can be pursued within it. Here are a few areas to consider that will be further developed in section two:

- *Distinct authority:* The common authority structure in a Southern Baptist Church is a single pastor model with varying aspects of authority unevenly distributed to deacons, committees, and the congregation. A common mark of a dying, divided church is a lack of clarity on who is in charge and, more importantly, who is supposed to be in charge.

- *Proper leadership:* When authority is unclear in a church, inevitably leaders are unclear on their role. When leadership fails to follow a biblical model a church cannot move towards church health. Church health, as well as a church for that matter, will rise and fall on its leaders, their roles, and a church's willingness to follow them.

- *Meaningful membership*: A common mark of a dying, divided church is the lack of an understanding of what it means to be a church member and the absence of any standard to become a member of the church. Since Southern Baptist Churches are congregational, it is imperative that the church know its members and the members understand what is expected of them as members of this covenant community.

- *Biblical knowledge:* If God's word is what the Spirit uses to breathe life into the church, then a church's basic knowledge of the Bible is essential. Churches that lost life throughout the decades frequently did so as a result of losing God's word in the Sunday school classes and pulpit. Somewhere down the line the church also lost its ears to hear.

- *Gospel clarity:* I once heard that a church that assumes the gospel, loses the gospel in the next generation.[2] This has become prophetic for many churches who once preached the gospel, only later to assume it and consequently lose it. A church that loses the gospel cannot experience true life or health. Gospel clarity is indispensable for new life for sinners and new growth for saints.

- *Love for one another:* A common mark of most churches needing revitalization is a church that is all one ethnicity and one generation. The body of Christ is to be a unified multi-generational and multi-ethnic church that demonstrates a deep sacrificial love for each other. Find that kind of diversity and love in one local church, and you will find marks of health.

- *Love for neighbor:* Although a common mistake is to look outward too quickly in revitalization work, loving those

---

2. I first heard this from Mark Dever, but it is explained in greater detail in Mack Stiles' book, *Marks of the Messenger* (Downers Grove: InterVarsity Press 2010), p. 40.

outside the church is essential not just to revitalize a church, but to establish a healthy church. Jesus said to love God and love our neighbor. This must be a part of the vision of the future if a church is to find life and flourish.

My goal as I went to pastor a church needing revitalization was to stay long enough to change the broken, dysfunctional patterns that had existed in the church for decades so as to establish healthier patterns that would not revert back once I left. These seven elements have major implications about structure and vision for a church to change an unhealthy culture to that which can thrive again. They show us how the glory of God can be seen in a church and thus provide a template for a pastor, regardless of the mess of a church, to know where to go.

How do I survive? (Personal Soul Care)

I wish I could say that most of my time caring for pastors is spent teaching them what to do and where to take a church over time, but it's not. Sadly, my time is mostly spent trying to get pastors to stay longer than a couple of years; trying to help pastors weather the difficult people, the criticisms, and the unmet expectations that lead to disappointment, even despair. Much of my effort is trying to keep a pastor's family from crumbling in the chaos of church life. There is a harsh reality in this fallen world that many of the labors of a pastor are incredibly hard, painful, and despairing. The work of revitalization only amplifies these struggles. This is one reason why Charles Spurgeon instructed his ministerial students to go and do something else if they could be happy doing it. Pastors need to know how to survive, but before I explain how a pastor prepares to survive in this work, allow me to address an unhelpful and unbiblical approach to survival in pastoral ministry.

Some seek ministry survival by finding what appears to be the easiest, most healthy church they can find to pastor. Some even use this 'easier road' as a reason to plant a church, thinking if I get to set the church up just like I want it from the beginning, I won't face many of the struggles of regular pastors. This is not a realistic understanding of pastoral ministry for several reasons. First, it is very unlikely a young man straight out of seminary will get that healthy church, even if it becomes available. Second, most pastors find that 'easier church' is still full of broken sinners and no pastoral ministry post is easy. An easier church post is not a good nor a biblical strategy for survival in pastoral ministry.

The key to survival in pastoral ministry is a pastor's diligent care for his own soul. Many of the discouragements that come in a pastor's ministry are about him, not his church. God calls pastors not to be supermen, but to be faithful. As pastors seek to be faithful every day in their ministries, God's sovereign will is being accomplished. Why is that not enough? Because a pastor brings with him to his church his own brokenness, personal struggles, and unhealed scars deep in his soul where God's grace in the gospel has yet to have an effect. Pastors struggle to find their true and full identity in Christ and when pastors fail to show up secure in Christ, they show up in these false ways:

- Insecure
- Defensive
- Controlling
- Perfectionistic
- Legalistic
- Fearing man
- Manipulative
- Passive
- Stoic
- Ungracious

These false ways of living expose the fact that a pastor is seeking the fulfillment that only Christ can provide and seeking it from the affirmation of others, his ministry successes, or self-imposed expectations. A powerful gospel-freeing truth for pastors who serve in difficult churches is that many discouragements come ultimately not from our church situation, but from crushing expectations we place on ourselves, people we fear and think we are responsible to change, and anxiety about how other 'more successful pastors' might evaluate our ministries. All this is about the pastor and his own soul—not the church. This turmoil that exists in every pastor's soul to some degree gets severely activated in church revitalization. Awareness of this needed soul work in every pastor is the answer to survival in the most difficult church scenario.

The gospel tells us our identity is in Christ. The Chief Shepherd reminds us our task is to shepherd His people until He returns for us (1 Pet. 5:4). When we as pastors realize that our worth and identity is found in Jesus, we are freed and secure to be who we are, live authentically, embrace our brokenness, emotionally connect, be gracious, love those who reject us, preach to those who hate our preaching, and lead in godly strength those who struggle to follow, knowing the Chief Shepherd is with us. Pastors have Jesus' approval, favor, and presence. What more do we need to survive? This is the key to survival in any church, but especially a church needing revitalization. A pastor's diligent care of his own soul and awareness of this needed internal work will be the key not just to survival, but thriving under the sovereign hand of the Chief Shepherd, regardless of the church he serves.

Should I revitalize a church? (The External Call)

There is plenty a man can do to prepare for the work of church revitalization. However, as this preparation takes place, how can a man know if he is fit and called for this difficult, but noble work? The answer is best summarized by an internal and external call. There is arguably no better work on the responsibility and the process for assessing God's calling than the writings of Charles Bridges (1794–1869). In Bridges's book, *The Christian Ministry*, he places the responsibility for the determination of one's call upon *both* the conscience of the individual and the local church to which he is committed. Bridges refers to these two aspects of calling as the *internal* and the *external* call of God:

> *The external call* is a commission received from and recognized by the Church, according to the sacred and primitive order; not indeed qualifying the Minister, but accrediting him, whom God had internally and suitably qualified. This call communicates therefore only official authority. *The internal call* is the voice and power of the Holy Ghost,

directing the will and the judgment, and conveying personal qualifications. Both calls, however—though essentially distinct in their character and source—are indispensable for the exercise of our commission.[3]

Bridges says that an individual must receive an internal call to know he is truly called of God to serve in the ministry. This is a God-given desire to do the work of the ministry combined with his own conviction that he has been gifted and empowered by God's Spirit to do this work.

In addition to the internal call, however, an individual must also possess an external call. This is the affirmation from a local church that he possesses the gifts and godly character suitable for a Christian minister. Bridges, Charles Spurgeon, and many other godly men whom God used in the past to prepare those called into the ministry all agree that *both* the internal and external calls are necessary for a person to enter into the work of the ministry.[4]

Unfortunately, few today experience this sort of dual calling. Over the last century the role of the local church and the importance of the external call have diminished, and one could argue that even the need for an internal call is seen as less important today as people treat pastoral ministry as just one career option among many. A recovery of the biblical teaching on these matters is urgently needed. This is especially true for those being trained to pastor a dying church, which is why the best way to train a man to go into a dying, divided church is to test, train, and affirm a man's gifts and calling while he observes another pastor serving in a similar type church he wishes to pastor. The process by which a local church grants an external call to a man seeking the work of revitalization is necessary to properly equip and prepare a man for this work.

If you are a man seeking this noble work to revitalize a church, prepare by placing yourself under the authority of a local church and leadership doing this work. Allow yourself to be tested and trained

---

3. Charles Bridges, *The Christian Ministry: An Inquiry into the Causes of its Inefficiency* (Edinburgh: Banner of Truth 1967), pp. 91-2.

4. I develop this idea more in my book, *Prepare Them To Shepherd: Test, Train, Affirm, and Send the Next Generation of Pastors* (Grand Rapids: Zondervan 2014).

by them. Have them assess your gifts, abilities, and calling. Follow them as they do the work of the ministry and shepherd God's people. Learn from them in the way they patiently and wisely move the structure of the church to a more biblical model over many years. Watch closely as the pastors walk with Jesus every day. Observe how they are able to absorb the criticisms and difficulties in a healthy way when their identity is secure in Christ, and how they struggle when it is not. Learn from their own personal soul work they do and may that soul work challenge you to walk in a more honest, broken, and authentic manner with Jesus now. Ultimately, prepare to pastor a dying church by growing to possess an unwavering confidence in who you are in Christ—for who you are in Christ is enough.

CHAPTER 3

PERSEVERANCE

How does a pastor persevere in revitalizing a church?

I AM regularly contacted by pastors commonly immersed in this scenario: caught in-between the eighteen/twenty-four-month mark. The honeymoon feels long gone. The enthusiastic pastoral committee members who hired him are now after him. Attendance has declined over those who have gotten mad and left. The preaching doesn't seem to be changing the people. A staff member has shown to be a nightmare. Intense discouragement has set in and the message I receive usually contains these words:

> I am very discouraged. My wife is done. Church leaders are frustrated with me. I am about to resign. Tell me why I shouldn't resign.

I find that these pastors in the midst of their discouragement lack two important things. First, they are unrealistic of what can be accomplished in the first few years. I often tell pastors at the two-year mark they have been there just long enough to realize what a mess of a church they took and the church has had just enough time to realize what a broken mess of a pastor they have. Second, pastors accept calls to churches and are not properly equipped with where their focus should be in those opening years. Whether going on a road trip, assembling a puzzle with your child, or accepting the call to pastor a dying church, it is incredibly valuable and empowering to know from the beginning those things that will remain constant and essential throughout the entire journey to get you to the end goal. Without them, pastors can make some costly early mistakes that can hinder a long-term fruitfulness.

This chapter considers what a pastor needs to know and understand to persevere in this work of revitalization *before* setting his hand to the plow. This chapter answers the question, How does a pastor persevere in revitalizing a church? But it is probably most helpful to consider this chapter as 'Eight strategies that can keep you from getting fired within the first two years at your church.'

1. Trust the Word

It is tempting for many pastors to look to modern gimmicks and pragmatism for the answer to bring life back to their struggling church. But the answer is the same as it was when Paul instructed Timothy to 'Preach the word' (2 Tim. 4:2). Only God by His Spirit through His word can breathe life into deadness. It is the same for the old, historic, established church about to close its doors. Pastors must preach and teach the word in such a way that they believe it is the only way God can breathe life back into a struggling congregation. A pastor must trust the power of the word in the preaching of the gospel to breathe life into the church. If he doesn't trust God's word, he will try and trust something else to bring life. If we believe God's word through His Spirit is what breathes life back into a dying and divided church, then the most important change comes the first Sunday of the new pastor. But time must be given for the word to do its work.

2. Shepherd souls

In so many cases, the decline and struggle of local churches can be traced to decades of unfaithful shepherds who cared more about numbers, programs, politics, and personal gain than the biblical call for pastors to shepherd the souls of God's people (1 Pet. 5:1-4; Heb. 13:17). Many churches needing revitalization have hurting, broken, discouraged sheep that need a shepherd to care for them and nurture them back to health. This is where a pastor's time needs to be spent as he seeks to be faithful, especially in the opening years of his ministry. If God is going to breathe life into His church, it must come through the revival of His people who are there. It is a common and costly error to immediately look outside the church for new life, when there are God's sheep longing for that renewed life already within the church.

3. Love all people

As we see the imperatives for pastors in Scripture to 'shepherd the flock' (1 Pet. 5:2) and to do so 'as those who will give an account' (Heb. 13:17), it is important to recognize that we don't get to pick who we will answer for in the church. It is tempting to conclude that a pastor will only answer for those who like him and gladly submit to his authority and ministry, but that is not the case. Often those are the members the pastor pursues and invests in during the early years. This is why a commitment to love all people in the church is essential to be faithful. Some in a church are more difficult to love than others, but the key to faithful revitalization is not just pouring into the teachable and supportive, but pursing those hard to love and seeking to win those who are cynical towards your ministry. Tell your people, show your people—all of them—that you love them. And do it often. The fruit of this labor comes much later, but it eventually becomes the sweetest fruit to taste.

4. Pray hard

The despair and discouragement that often accompany dying, divided churches can create a panicked approach that could lead pastors to act hastily and think they have to solve every problem now. Sometimes the best thing to do to be faithful in a struggling church is to stop and pray and cry out to God for your church and your people. The despair of church revitalization can wire us to try and solve the financial crisis, instead of just praying for God to provide. It can cause us to quickly remove leaders instead of praying that God would intervene and mature that leader. If we truly believe that God is the one who breathes life into a dying church, not our clever schemes in the church, we better make sure we find ourselves on our knees crying to the Chief Shepherd who loves our church more than we do. In my experience, rarely has a pastor ready to bail at the two-year mark prayed as he ought for his flock.

5. Celebrate older members

If a church has been around for many years, inevitably there are long term older members still in these churches who long for their church to return to its former glory. These are typically the ones who have kept the struggling church open for many years, but are also the ones who are commonly resistant to needed change. Because of this, these longtime faithful members can appear to be more of a hindrance for renewed life instead of a benefit. Faithfulness in revitalization is to take these long term members, love and accept them where they are, and find ways to celebrate them.

It is all too common for a young pastor to walk into a church and conclude these older members are the problem and therefore the solution is to run them out. But God reveals His design for the local church to have both old and young in the church (Titus 2:1-8). Faithfulness requires a pastor to love the older members in the congregation and realize he needs them in a revitalization work if that church is to reflect God's design. If a pastor will find ways to celebrate these long-term faithful saints that have kept that church going when everyone else bailed out, it will cause them to be most receptive to the younger, who also need to come to the church for the church to survive into the next generation.

6. Be patient

In the early years of revitalization work pastors are often convinced they—in contrast to their members who are so resistant to change— are the patient ones. Many pastors have thought this at one time or another in their revitalization efforts in the face of criticism, conflicts, and attacks on their ministries. Pastors think they are being more patient and faithful than the church members. As the years pass, pastors realize in a lot of ways that it was the other way around. These long-time faithful saints wounded by previous pastors for decades were the ones being patient. They were being patient as the pastor grew in his preaching. They were being patient as the new pastor learned to love them. They were patient through the pastor's rookie mistakes. They were patient through all the changes they did not understand or agree with.

The longer a pastor endures, is patient, and stays, the greater will become his realization that he was shown much grace. Patience might be the most important key to perseverance as it will cause a pastor to wait when he needs to wait. It will cause a pastor to make decisions with a longer view in mind. Patience will cause a pastor to not give up on a difficult person just yet. Patience is not just a significant fruit of the spirit in every Christian's life, but a key element to both surviving and avoiding great discouragement. And if that is not persuasive enough, let us be reminded that patience is commanded of the pastor, 'I solemnly charge you in the presence of God and of Christ Jesus, who is to judge the living and the dead, and by His appearing and His kingdom: preach the word; be ready in season and out of season; reprove, rebuke, exhort, *with great patience* and instruction' (2 Tim. 4:1-2, italics added). Patience is essential for a pastor to persevere in this work.

7. Expect suffering

If you are a pastor trying to revitalize a church holding on to the hope suffering will not come, you should find another line of work now. In many cases, the reason pastors are ready to resign after about two years of ministry in one place is because they finally met the adversaries the enemy had placed there in that open door of ministry. As many pastors begin to talk through the discouragement and struggles, we eventually ask them, 'Did you think becoming the pastor of that church would not bring with it adversaries to come against your gospel ministry?'

Ironically, in many cases it is their confrontation with adversaries against the gospel and their ministries that make them conclude it is time for the next place. The Apostle Paul takes the opposite approach—the presence of adversaries makes him conclude he must stay longer:

> But I will remain in Ephesus until Pentecost; for a wide door for effective service has opened to me, and there are many adversaries (1 Cor. 16:8-9).

Becoming a pastor means we place our families and ourselves on the front lines of spiritual battle. Why are pastors so surprised when the enemy comes against our gospel ministry, especially in places it has been suppressed for decades? Charles Simeon said, 'Brothers we must not mind a little suffering.' Expect suffering in this work of revitalization so when it does come, you will not be shocked and preparation for this suffering can lead to your perseverance through it.

8. Pick battles wisely

A key to a soldier's survival on the battlefield is to know there are land mines out there and do whatever he must to avoid stepping on them. The work of revitalization is similar in that you can survive a long time if you can avoid stepping on those giant landmines, know what they are, and identify when they are near. There are plenty of battles to fight. The key is knowing what needs to be fought now and what needs to wait. This is essential to perseverance.

Even when you step on one, God will use it to give you discernment to know what battles to fight tomorrow. God in His sovereign grace uses the worst moments in our ministries to bring a unique perspective in a pastor's life like nothing else once real revitalizing change occurs. The trials a pastor endures in his church can bring a perspective in decision-making that few in the church will have. This perspective allows a special wisdom and discernment to choose battles wisely.

So when our newest young member has just discovered 9 Marks Ministries and is really uptight about those eight to ten members on the fringe, or those family members of long time church members still on the rolls, he does not remember the blood, sweat, tears, and bruises that came to remove hundreds of 'inactive' members a few years prior. He does not know about the finger-pointing threat received in the deacons' meeting five years earlier that started the conversation. God grows a unique discernment and wisdom in a pastor through the pastoral scars of the journey. Nothing can serve a pastor as well as the wisdom wrought by scars. Those scars will bring wisdom and that wisdom is a key to persevere in this work.[1]

Church revitalization is a long hard work. It cannot be done in a few years. It requires a man called by God not just to go to a dying church, but to go, plant, stay, wait, and be patient. No one will approach this long, hard, but noble work in a fruitful way if their ambition is to conquer the world in two years. Nor will a man bear lasting fruit if he is not equipped with that which will give him a vision for what to do from the beginning and how to press on. In many ways, persevering in the work of revitalization comes by what you know, understand, and expect before going. Never lose sight that the road to long term, faithful perseverance begins before the work even starts.

---

1. I further develop these eight strategies in Mohler (ed.), *A Guide to Church Revitalization.*

CHAPTER 4

PLAN

How is church revitalization accomplished?

THIS unprecedented need to revitalize struggling churches has produced a plethora of ways and philosophies to accomplish it. There are many strategies and each strategist is convinced he has the right formula. These varying methods typically market well since many of these approaches promise quick and reproducible results. The approach I am advocating in this book, however, will not sweep the church growth executives off their feet. It will not launch the next pragmatic program trend. It will not cause Twitter to explode, nor will it gain a mass following among seminarians desiring to be successful pastors inside of five years. No, this plan is different.

The biblical approach to true, life-giving church revitalization that will remain throughout future generations will take a long time. It will be hard. It will involve difficult shepherding work that in many cases only you and God will know about. It will be a significant challenge for your family. Now before you consider me the worst recruiter of young pastors to engage in the work of church revitalization, allow me to submit to you why this plan is the best and most effective way of breathing new life into a struggling church. First, this approach is firmly rooted in the principles taught in Scripture specifically about church revitalization. Second, this approach is predicated on the power of God to work through His word to bring true, lasting spiritual life to a local church.

This chapter captures the plan. It is a plan that balances the Pragmatist and the Purist. It is a plan that allows Scripture to be the guiding force of the work, but also provides room to be thoughtful, creative, and eager to use the gifts of those involved. The biblical plan is this—a central focus on the ministry of the word and prayer, a rigorous and passionate application of the gospel in everyday life, and a tenacious effort to love and shepherd every redeemed soul in that local church.

Centrality of the word and prayer

It is stunning how many feel that a vibrant church full of life must have a pastor with a big personality, highly efficient programs, plenty of money, and a breath-taking modern facility. But the New Testament paints a very different picture. The infant church grew and was nourished by two fundamental commitments of the Apostles: prayer and the ministry of the word (Acts 6:4). These two essential means of grace for revitalization compel the consciences of churches to surrender their clever efforts unto God's all-wise and powerful plan.

This approach continues in the Pastoral Epistles where the Apostle Paul writes to his young protégé, Timothy. In the midst of exhorting Timothy to trust the 'sacred writings' which are able to give both wisdom and salvation in Jesus (2 Tim. 3:15) for the churches Timothy is establishing, Paul then adds:

> All Scripture is inspired by God and profitable for teaching,
> for reproof, for correction, for training in righteousness; so

that the man of God may be adequate, equipped for every
good work (2 Tim. 3:16-17).

In these inspired writings of the Apostle to his young protégé, who is himself pastoring the church in Ephesus, there exists a template for God's design to breathe life into His church through His inspired word.

Paul wants Timothy to know that God's word is 'God-breathed'. Paul writes that, 'All scripture is *inspired* by God.' Most translations word it in this way, but the literal meaning here is 'God-breathed'. All Scripture has been breathed from the very mouth of God. God so identifies with His word that when Scripture speaks, God Himself speaks. God is perfectly righteous and holy in all His ways. Likewise, God's breathed word is perfect, holy, and without error or flaw. If God is the one who gives life, then it is His Spirit, working through His divine, God-breathed word that gives life to our souls and consequently genuine life to a church.

God's word is profitable to teach us the truth. *Teaching* refers to the divine instruction that the word of God brings. *Reproof* is the word's ability to pierce the sinful heart, revealing wrong behavior that needs to be changed. The *corrective* aspect of God's word empowers that change in our lives. Because the word of God is God-breathed, using it for *training in righteousness* allows us to be instructed by God. The pastor need not wonder what to tell his flock about how to live a godly life, for the God-breathed word is his all-sufficient manual. Similarly, it is the tool needed for the man of God to be equipped for every good work. So then, it should not surprise us that after Paul lifts up the power and sufficiency of God's word he issues the central imperative for Timothy as well as all pastors: 'Preach the word!' (4:2).[1]

And yet, we must not miss the essential need to cry out to God in prayer as we preach the word. The Apostles knew that 'prayer and the ministry of the word' together must encapsulate their calling

---

1. 2 Timothy 4:1 is one of the most unhelpful chapter breaks in all of Scripture, for it obscures the connection between the sufficiency of the word and the proclamation of the word. Chapter divisions were added to the Bible in the thirteenth century A.D. as a means of navigating the biblical text and are not inspired.

and priority. Paul recognized that prayer was an essential element in promoting the work of sanctification in the life of the believer. That is why he prayed for the Ephesian Christians in this way:

> For this reason I bow my knees before the Father, from whom every family in heaven and on earth derives its name, that He would grant you, according to the riches of His glory, to be strengthened with power through His Spirit in the inner man, so that Christ may dwell in your hearts through faith; and that you, being rooted and grounded in love, may be able to comprehend with all the saints what is the breadth and length and height and depth, and to know the love of Christ which surpasses knowledge, that you may be filled up to all the fullness of God (Eph. 3:14-19).

Paul offers similar prayers for the churches in Philippi (Phil. 1:9-11) and in Colossae (Col. 1:9-12). If this was important for an apostle praying for believers in distant churches, how much more so for a pastor in the local church? If you want your people to become more Christ-like, you must pray for them. If you are to care for them as a shepherd cares for the sheep, you must pray for them. Instead of becoming impatient when your flock is not growing in grace at the pace you had hoped, employ the means that God has provided you with as their pastor for their sanctification. Let your heart's frustration become your heart's prayer for your people. The centrality of the ministry of the word must be bathed in prayer for it to have its maximum impact on God's people and bring true, lasting spiritual life to the church.

Application of the Gospel
The power of the good news of Jesus is best captured by the one whose life was dramatically transformed by it. The Apostle Paul, formally a persecutor of Christians himself, writes:

> For I am not ashamed of the gospel, for it is the power of God for salvation to everyone who believes, to the Jew first and also to the Greek (Rom. 1:16).

Divine power—that is what is needed to breathe life into a spiritual corpse. Only power from God can change the heart of a thief, a murderer, and the sexually immoral. Only a supernatural work from God can take a hater of God who is dead in his sins and transform him into a lover of God who is alive because of righteousness. Only divine power brings about forgiveness, eternal life, and spiritual adoption. If this is true for individual sinners who trust in Christ, then it is no less true for the church. Supernatural power is needed to bring life into a seemingly dead church. This life comes through a passionate, right application of the gospel in a church as we preach, apply, and live out that gospel.

Pastors must first preach the gospel for the gospel to be heard. It is preached for the believer who has come on Sunday so that we might be reminded of the hope we have in Christ. It is also preached for the unbeliever who may be present, for 'Faith comes by hearing and hearing by the word of Christ' (Rom. 10:17). The gospel is 'the power of God for salvation to everyone who believes.' It empowers the unbeliever to believe and the believer to be strengthened in his faith. That is why we never stop preaching the gospel.

This regular preaching of the gospel for all present on a Sunday has its power in two ways. First, the gospel's power is experienced when the essentials of it are made known. Pastors need to preach not only the cross but also the resurrection. Pastors must preach not just the sinlessness of Jesus, but also His righteousness that is imputed to us by faith through His perfect life. It is an unbalanced gospel if we do not preach both the wrath of God and the mercy of God in the cross. The power of the gospel is experienced when these specific details are highlighted and made regularly known in a church.

Second, the gospel's power is known when we preach it throughout the texts of the Old and New Testaments. The gospel permeates the full redemptive story of the Bible. As a pastor preaches through different passages of Scripture, it is a powerful experience to see how that Old Testament passage points forward to the coming Messiah, or how that letter from an Apostle points back to the significance of the cross. There is always power when the gospel is declared in its simplest form, but there is a unique power that breathes life into a dying church when that gospel is preached in certain ways week after week that moves it to become the heartbeat of a local church.

A faithful pastor must deliberately and continually teach his people that the gospel is what transforms all aspects of their lives. A traveling evangelist can preach the gospel in its basic form, lead a soul to Christ, plug them into a local church, and then leave for the next preaching post. But a pastor of a local church has the responsibility to help a congregation learn how to take this life-giving good news and apply it to their everyday lives. Jesus died for your sins. You have forgiveness and the promise of eternal life with Jesus. You have been reconciled to God. While all these things are true, the question is, 'So what?' How do these truths affect your daily life now? A shepherd should never assume his sheep understand how to accomplish this. Failing to connect these dots can be part of the reason a once vibrant local church loses its way. This pastoral application starts with specific applications in the weekly sermons based on the text a pastor preaches. Our preaching should address specific ways the gospel transforms relationships with spouses and children. It should declare how to be faithful to Jesus at work and with our neighbors. It should lead believers to freedom from the bondages of perfectionism and legalism as they embrace their brokenness, weakness, and sin, knowing that Jesus' sacrifice has paid the price for all these. A congregation who knows the gospel and has been taught how it should bear fruit in their daily lives will be a church equipped to live the gospel out.

Living out this good news is evidenced in the way Christians show love and mercy to all kinds of different people regardless of race, gender, or social class; it is seen in the love Christians have for one another; it is known in the kind and encouraging words that come from our mouths towards our adversaries; it is displayed in the way we share the gospel with neighbors and take the gospel to the nations. If these are just a few of the manifestations of living out the gospel, imagine what life is breathed into a struggling church if these kinds of people living out the gospel are found in it. A right and passionate application of the gospel in the lives of Christ's redeemed people is enough to radically change a dying church and give it new life, for it is the gospel that is 'the power of God for salvation to everyone who believes.'

Shepherd every redeemed soul

It is unfortunate the amount of dying churches that conclude they need one of two kinds of men to lead them to revitalize their church. Some churches search for the next young, rock-star preacher to be their pastor, banking that his charisma will be what breathes life back into the church. The problem with this approach is not just the limited amount of so called rock-star pastors that exist, but that the Bible does not promote such characteristics for men who lead the church. Other churches look for a fiery evangelist who will go out into the community and win souls for Jesus. This is supposed to help the church grow and consequently bring fresh new life. Neither of these is what is necessary for God to revitalize a struggling church.

So what is necessary? What does God want? He simply wants faithful shepherds. God wants men who meet certain qualifications and have godly character (1 Tim. 3:1-7; Titus 1:5-9). God wants a humble, eager man who is called to shepherd the flock of God on behalf of the Chief Shepherd (1 Pet. 5:1-4). God wants pastors who realize their calling is to take heed to themselves and to the flock that Christ purchased with His own blood (Acts 20:28). God wants faithful shepherds who are not defined by their cleverness or charisma, but by a divine conviction to care for souls because they will give an account to Jesus for them (Heb. 13:17).

Many approaches to revitalization challenge dying congregations set in their ways to look outward for new life. I am not discouraging evangelistic efforts, but if God has sheep already in a local church we should begin there and not be so quick to try and replace them as the solution. Too often the decline of local churches has come as a result of the progression of neglectful, unfaithful shepherds. Throughout decades of neglect the spiritual life in the sheep of the church slowly dwindles to a mere ember. But there is spiritual life in all true followers of Jesus, regardless of how beat up and discouraged they may be. Christ still lives in them and is working to complete the work He began (Phil. 1:6).

God desires faithful shepherds to care for the flock. He breathes life into the church when His sheep are well cared for. There are many facets to pastors who care for their people. But here are a few priorities driven by a ministry of the word and prayer that should be focused on to shepherd every redeemed soul in the church and help fan into flame that ember in the hearts of God's people who remain:[2]

- Visit the sick and dying
- Comfort the grieving
- Care for widows
- Confront sin
- Encourage the weaker sheep

When a pastor first focuses inward to care well for his present flock, often that fresh new life God brings in that present flock draws those from the outside who want to come and share in the same spiritual life.

Here is one final reality that assures that every redeemed soul in a struggling church receives proper care. As a pastor sets out to shepherd the remnant of God's sheep in a church that needs revitalization, he must arm himself with the truth that the residual effects of the failings of previous pastors are still felt in his congregation. The hurt and pain a previous pastor caused a congregation does not vanish when the new pastor arrives. And here's the difficult truth: you, as the new pastor, should expect to suffer because of them. You will pay the price and bear the burden for the failings of your predecessors. It is neither fair nor right, but that's the reality.

So what does this mean for you? You must shepherd the souls of everyone, not just those who like you and support your ministry from the beginning. You must shepherd all the sheep God gives you. This includes the sheep that are hard to love and the sheep that dislike your preaching and approach to ministry. A pastor may face wolves in sheep's clothing, unbelievers within his church. That is another matter that Scripture clearly addresses. But be careful about quickly dismissing opposition as unbelief. It may instead be

---

2. These priorities are explained in greater detail in my book, *The Pastor's Ministry: Biblical priorities for faithful shepherds* (Grand Rapids: Zondervan 2015).

wounded sheep simply struggling to trust the next shepherd. Be patient with them. They, more than anyone, need the loving and patient care of a faithful shepherd. Start on the inside with the sheep that remain. Otherwise what kind of church will the new arrivals that you go and get from the community find?

Churches that desire true spiritual life in their church must seek it from God. God has revealed in and through His word where that lasting power and life comes from. It comes when we cry out to God in prayer to move and we preach the only divine word that breathes life in the church. It comes when the gospel is not just preached and made known, but its truths permeate every crevice and corner of the church. It comes not through the most gifted pastor, but through a faithful one who leads and functions in his daily ministry as if he will give an account for souls, not large crowds or fancy buildings. God is able to breathe life into any dying and divided church. The question is whether God's people trust He is powerful enough to do it His way—and will follow His plan.

Section II:
Church Revitalization –
Diagnosed

Chapter 5

AUTHORITY

Who is in charge?

IT was a cold Wednesday evening when I walked into this struggling church. A young, eager pastor greeted me at the door of the meeting room and introduced me to the committee. They were a friendly group, but timid. Most were older—long time pillars of the church. All were white. The committee had formed because the church realized that something was not right. They needed a change, but weren't sure what that was. They knew the church was broken, but didn't know how to fix it. I had been invited to this first of what would be numerous meetings of a church revitalization committee. My role was to help prepare them to walk through whatever revitalization would look like for them.

The first thing that this group needed to do was honestly assess where the church was in its current state. Not what it once was, not what they wished it was, but a realistic and accurate appraisal of where the church was right then and how it might have gotten there. I presented five areas to them to help them think clearly through that process of evaluation. Evaluating these five areas are crucial to every congregation if it is to navigate the revitalization process well.

This chapter addresses what is the first and arguably most important of these five areas—authority. The first question I asked in that committee meeting was, 'Who's in charge?' Let me be clear on what I am asking. I am not asking who the by-laws say is in charge. I am not asking who moderates the business meetings or leads the deacons' meetings. I am asking, Who has the greatest influence in the church? Who do church members go to when decisions need to be made? Who do church members listen to the most? Just because a pastor gets paid a full-time salary and preaches every week doesn't make him the man in charge. You must first determine where the authority in the church really lies. Only then can you compare your answer to Scripture's answer.

There is a key passage that reveals important aspects of the authority structure of a New Testament church and it is found in a letter the Apostle Peter wrote where he exhorts pastors to be faithful in their appointed task from God:

> Therefore, I exhort the elders among you, as your fellow elder and witness of the sufferings of Christ, and a partaker also of the glory that is to be revealed, shepherd the flock of God among you, exercising oversight not under compulsion, but voluntarily, according to the will of God; and not for sordid gain, but with eagerness; nor yet as lording it over those allotted to your charge, but proving to be examples to the flock. And when the Chief Shepherd appears, you will receive the unfading crown of glory (1 Pet. 5:1-4).

The Bible is clear about who is in charge: Jesus Christ. Peter calls Him the Chief Shepherd (1 Pet. 5:4). His authority is mediated to us through His word. If a church willingly submits to the authority of Christ, there is no confusion about where the final word lies.

Peter also gives guidance about those to whom that authority is given. Pastors (elders) are exhorted to shepherd the flock exercising oversight (v. 2). Pastors accomplish this by the authority of Christ through the means of His written word. They exercise oversight in a godly humble manner on behalf of the Chief Shepherd until He returns for His people. Committees, deacons, trustees, and Bible study teachers all play an important role in a local church. But none of these are called to exercise oversight for the Chief Shepherd as those who will give any account (Heb. 13:17). Only pastors are given that charge. In light of this template which Peter gives us, the basic authority structure in a local church is clear:

God

Authority begins and ends with the Creator of the Universe (Gen. 1–2), the all-wise and all-knowing God (Rom. 11:33-36). Paul describes him to Timothy as the 'King eternal, immortal, invisible, the only God … (1 Tim. 1:17)'. God the Father rules on high and answers to no one. It is God who is the supreme authority and only ruler in the universe. All authority structures must begin and end with the Lord Most High, especially His church made up of His redeemed people.

Jesus Christ

He is the Son of God (1 John 1:3), the Chief Shepherd (1 Pet. 5:4), our Great High Priest (Heb. 9:11), the sufficient sacrifice for our sins (Heb. 10:10), and the one to whom the Father and ruler of the universe has given all authority (Matt. 28:18-20). Jesus now rules on behalf of the Father at His right hand and this includes His bride, the church. Jesus' perfect life, atoning death, and glorious resurrection that brought salvation to God's people has uniquely qualified Him to rule over humanity and all the nations of the earth.

God's word

The person and work of Jesus Christ and His authority are now known and revealed through His inerrant, infallible word, the Bible. Through His word we see and know Jesus' authority over all things. Through His word pastors are thoroughly equipped with everything needed to be ministers of the power and grace of the gospel to the church and world. God's word is living and active (Heb. 4:12), inspired by God and profitable for teaching, reproof, correction and training in righteousness (2 Tim. 3:16), and is to be preached in the presence of God and of Christ Jesus in season and out of season (2 Tim. 4:1-2).

Pastors

Pastors are biblically qualified leaders (1 Tim. 3:1-7; Titus 1:5-9), appointed by God to be the under-shepherds of the Chief Shepherd (1 Pet. 5:1-2) to minister God's word to himself and God's redeemed people (1 Tim. 4:16) and to protect the flock (Acts 20:28), all of which is accomplished with patience, grace, and humility (1 Pet. 5:2-3) and a knowledge that they will give an account to the Chief Shepherd for the flock under their care (Heb. 13:17). Pastors do not have any authority in and of themselves, but only that which is given by God, through God's word, on behalf of the Chief Shepherd.

Congregation

The congregation possessing authority in an autonomous local church is arguably the most unique mark of Southern Baptist Churches and its polity structure. Most of the biblical evidence of this polity structure is found in the congregation's authority to discipline and restore those in the church. Jesus establishes a process to confront sin with the whole church as the final step to removal (Matt. 18:15-17). Paul confronts the members of the Corinthian church for not removing some in their midst who were involved in gross, public sin (1 Cor. 5:2). The clearest biblical evidence pointing to the congregational voting process for which Baptist churches are known comes from Paul's instruction to the Corinthian church regarding one who had been removed from the church by a determination of 'the majority' (2 Cor. 2:6). This final authority in matters of local church life is given with the understanding of a willing submission to the authority of the pastors, God's word, and ultimately God the Father and His Son, Jesus Christ.

Most churches have other supplemental roles to whom some form of authority is given. Examples include staff, deacons, committees, trustees, children's workers, and many others. In light of this a local church needs to evaluate its authority structure to determine whether someone or some group in the church has been given an authority unwarranted from Scripture.

For example, churches that have lost life and become hostile towards each other and divided commonly had pastors at some point that abused their authority. They had leaders that decided to rely on the wisdom of the world instead of the truth of God's word. In the absence of strong, godly pastoral leadership, other less qualified leaders or committee members took that authority over time and did not steward the Chief Shepherd's given authority properly. Over time congregations lose sight of the fact that their authority given from above is for the sake of purity in the church, not so everyone can get their individual say on every matter in the church.

Every church needing revitalization can assume at some point in the ups and downs of their existence that they lost sight of this biblical model and structure of authority and must begin to recover it if any other patterns of dysfunction can be addressed to ensure a healthy direction for the future. Authority matters. Who is in charge in your church? Jesus is the bridegroom of His bride. He is in charge. He is the one to whom the church must submit if it is to have life and experience the unity that only He can bring, for it came at the cost of His own life (Eph. 2:11-15).

CHAPTER 6

LEADERSHIP
Whom do I follow?

WHEN I arrived as Senior Pastor of our church, I was eager to build relationships with the leadership and see who the congregation was following. I was amazed to find it wasn't a pastor or deacon. Nor was it an influential Bible study teacher or committee head. The one everyone followed was the elderly secretary. As I inquired further I discovered there had been a string of pastors who had stayed for only two to three years, but the one constant that remained was this lady's tenure. She had been in this staff role of secretary for over a decade when I arrived. In the absence of strong, consistent leadership, the church looked to the next best thing, which was a faithful, but old, frail, elderly lady whose health was fading. Nevertheless, she ran the church and everybody knew it.

It is essential to assess who the leaders are in the church. Churches within my denomination have experienced an epidemic of short pastorates. One consequence of this tragedy is the creation of an environment in which church members have had to assume roles of leadership spawned by the vacuum of leadership during the absence of a pastor. To be clear, the problem is not with filling roles of leadership during the absence of a pastor. The problem is what happens to it once the church has a pastor. The revolving door cycle of short term pastorates creates a breeding ground in which churches, too frequently burned, come to distrust the pastoral office, albeit unknowingly and allow others to usurp leadership roles. Every church must realistically consider who the church is truly following. Only then can a more biblical paradigm be taught and pursued.

This chapter addresses this second area of leadership that must be evaluated in every church and is summarized by this question, Whom do I follow? This area is very closely tied to the first area of authority. Even if a biblical understanding of authority is adopted, without proper, qualified leadership to carry out that paradigm, the church cannot move to a greater place of health. Similar to authority, God gives a very clear pattern in the New Testament of those who are uniquely and divinely called to lead Christ's bride. That pattern consists of two and only two biblical offices of the church: pastors and deacons.

Most Baptist churches are faithful to have in some form the presence of these two separate offices. Where they often deviate from a more biblical pattern is in both the qualifications and func-tions of these offices. The Bible presents clear qualifications of pastors and deacons and the proper roles of each (1 Tim. 3:1-13; 1 Pet. 5:1-4; Titus 1:5-9; Heb. 13:17). The Apostle Paul gives to Timothy clear, specific qualifications for those who are to hold these biblical offices:

> It is a trustworthy statement: if any man aspires to the office
> of overseer, it is a fine work he desires to do. An overseer,

then, must be above reproach, the husband of one wife, temperate, prudent, respectable, hospitable, able to teach, not addicted to wine or pugnacious, but gentle, peaceable, free from the love of money. He must be one who manages his own household well, keeping his children under control with all dignity (but if a man does not know how to manage his own household, how will he take care of the church of God?), and not a new convert, so that he will not become conceited and fall into the condemnation incurred by the devil. And he must have a good reputation with those outside the church, so that he will not fall into reproach and the snare of the devil.

Deacons likewise must be men of dignity, not double-tongued, or addicted to much wine or fond of sordid gain, but holding to the mystery of the faith with a clear conscience. These men must also first be tested; then let them serve as deacons if they are beyond reproach. Women must likewise be dignified, not malicious gossips, but temperate, faithful in all things. Deacons must be husbands of only one wife, and good managers of their children and their own households. For those who have served well as deacons obtain for themselves a high standing and great confidence in the faith that is in Christ Jesus (1 Tim. 3:1-13).

Faithfulness to the biblical paradigm involves having not only the offices, but a proper understanding of them as well. Each is distinct from the other. Paul writes that the office of an overseer, or pastor, is 'a fine work he desires to do' (v. 1). Paul ends this section with these words in regard to a deacon who serves well, 'obtains for themselves a high standing and great confidence in the faith that is in Christ Jesus (v. 13).' Sandwiched between these bookends is Paul's description of the person that qualifies for these particular offices in the church. Many of these characteristics only lay the foundation of a godly, holy life that is to be displayed in its fullest by those God has called to these two offices. There exists biblical evidence of the similarities of these two offices as well as what makes these offices distinct from one another in God's all-wise design.

Similar Qualifications[1]

- Blameless Reputation

The pastor and deacon are firmly called to this qualification. The strongest evidence of this is the qualification of being 'above reproach' (1 Tim. 3:2, 10[2]). This entails not just fleeing from evil, but fleeing from even the appearance of evil. For example, it is very hard to accuse a pastor of having an affair if everyone knows he will not be alone in a room with another woman except his wife. Pastors and deacons are to live above any accusations by means of their consistent godly life displayed to all people. They are not to be in bondage to any substance, but self-controlled which seems to be why Paul mentions for a pastor and deacon to 'not be addicted to wine' (vv. 3, 8). Paul even insists upon a testing period for the deacon (v. 10) to confirm their irreproachable lifestyle. Pastors are to have a good reputation with those outside the church (v. 7). Pastors and deacons are to live honest, authentic lives before the church and the world. A blameless reputation does not in any way demand perfectionism, but a transparent life of a faithful person who is above accusation.

- Manager of Home

The main components of this qualification are for a man to be faithful to his wife (vv. 2, 12) and care for his children well (vv. 4, 12). The reason for this important qualification is also given: 'If a man does not know how to manage his own household well, how will he take care of the church of God?' (v. 5). How one manages his home, when used rightly, can be an accurate gauge of how well he will manage other things, including his responsibilities in the church. God's design for the home and church is implied in these verses, that the role of husband, father, pastor, and deacon are to be played by qualified men.

---

1. These ideas are further developed in my book, *Prepare Them to Shepherd: test, train, affirm, and send the next generation*.

2. Though verse 10 is a different word in the original (v. 2 *anepilēmptos*, v. 10 *anegklētos*), the same concept is in view. See also Titus 1:6-7 where *anegklētos* is used of elders.

- Godly Character

Most of these characteristics listed by Paul could fall into a category of godly character. But there are a few that point specifically to the transformation of the gospel shown to others. The pastor is to be temperate, prudent, and respectable (v. 2). The pastor is to be gentle and not contentious (v. 3). The deacon similarly is to be a man of dignity (v. 8) and not double-tongued (v. 8). All of these qualities speak of the fruit of the Spirit, an inward transformation of the gospel displayed in kindness, compassion, and being self-controlled with words and actions.

- Spiritual Maturity

Despite the fact that much of this list could also fall under this heading, there seem to be two specific qualities that evidence true spiritual maturity. The first is that pastors and deacons are to be free from a love for money and the things of the world (vv. 3, 8). The pastor's primary responsibility is to preach and teach God's word and the things of God. Therefore, it would be a contradiction if the pastor was being faithful to his call and money was an idol in his life. This naturally applies to deacons also as they handle church resources and finances in a variety of ways in serving the church.

Secondly, as the spiritual leader of the church, the pastor cannot be a new convert (v. 6), which also implies that a spiritually immature man should not be a pastor. Paul gives an important reason—so he does not become conceited (v. 6). An immature believer could get caught up in the power of the position instead of seeing the pastoral office as a place of sacrifice and service to God and His people. A deacon having a strong and mature faith is what Paul is describing when he writes of a deacon, 'Holding to the mystery of the faith with a clear conscience' (v. 9).

- Plurality

Although not explicitly stated by Paul to Timothy, it is consistently implied all throughout the New Testament that there is to be more than one pastor and deacon in each local church. Other than the passages that describe the qualifications of a pastor or deacon (1 Tim. 3:1-13; Titus 1:5-9) there are numerous examples of both these offices serving with other qualified men, sharing the responsibilities (Acts 20:28; 1 Pet. 5:1-4; Heb. 13:17). Not to mention, the burdens and responsibilities of these two offices are too great for one man to carry alone.

Distinct Qualifications:

- Teaching vs. Well-taught

Paul's list to Timothy demonstrates one main distinction that is significant to understanding the different roles of these two offices: the pastor is to be able to teach (v. 2). The pastor's calling is one of preaching and teaching God's word in such a way that guards the good deposit of the gospel that is entrusted to this office (2 Tim. 1:14). Though we have a narrative account in Acts 8 of a deacon who instructed others in the faith, nowhere does Scripture require public teaching as a responsibility of a deacon. Holding fast to the clear teachings of the faith is required of both pastors (Titus 1:9) and deacons (1 Tim. 3:9), the implied reason being that neither would swerve from gospel faithfulness. But the added reasons of exhortation and refutation of false teaching are applied only to the pastor.

- Oversight vs. Service

The office of a pastor is also referred to as 'an overseer' (v. 1), which captures well another distinct role from the role of a deacon. Peter affirms this distinction as he exhorts his fellow elders (pastors) to shepherd the flock by 'exercising oversight' eagerly, sacrificially, and humbly (1 Pet. 5:2-3). A deacon's primary role is that of service. This is not to say that deacons do not oversee certain ministries, nor does this imply that pastors should not serve. But this refers to the primary biblical role of each office where the pastors exercise oversight (lead, oversee, administrate) over all matters within the local church and the deacons lead in service, under the submission of the pastors.

- Shepherding vs. Practical Doing

Peter exhorts the elders (pastors) regarding their primary calling— shepherding the flock (1 Pet. 5:2). The office of a pastor is an extension of the care of the Chief Shepherd (1 Pet. 5:4). Most of the qualifications of the pastor (1 Tim. 3:1-7) demonstrate the heart of a shepherd who should be willing to lay down his life for his flock. Although there is shepherding involved in the role of a deacon at times, the primary gifts needed in a deacon are one of skill sets that allow a deacon to serve in a variety of roles that fill the unique and pressing physical needs of a church. Though the men selected to serve the widows by the Apostles in Acts 6:1-7 are not called deacons, they present a helpful proto-type of the role of deacons that is established later in the church. Ultimately, deacons will not give an account to the Chief Shepherd for the souls of their flock—the office of the pastor is the only office that assumes this weighty, joyful burden (1 Pet. 5:1-4; Heb. 13:17).

Churches that lose their way and eventually forfeit spiritual vibrancy often do so as a result of a sloppy evaluation of those who would step up to serve in these two biblical offices. When a church stops vetting those who would serve as pastors and deacons and those roles become filled by those who are unqualified, death is imminent. Many of the churches that need revitalization have deacons or committee heads who assumed the authority of the pastoral office in the absence of faithful, consistent men. Unqualified staff may temporarily be utilized to fill a gap, but those roles must be passed to the next leader whose role it truly is to play. When unqualified men step into the pulpit, the treasure of the gospel that has been entrusted to pastors is not guarded as Scripture prescribes.

For a dying, divided church to find life again, it must know who to follow. It isn't the family who has been there the longest or has given the most money to the building campaign. It isn't the staff person who has the longest tenure. God's design is for there to be two offices of pastors and deacons; two offices distinct from each other, both of which know their roles and seek to serve in them with all their might. There are all kinds of leaders in the local church. They are called many things—committee heads, trustees, bible study teachers, team leaders, coordinators, administrators, and secretaries, to name a few. But title, influence, and salary do not change their responsibility that even they follow the shepherding and oversight of the pastors and the service and leadership of the deacons. My experience has been that when godly, gifted, qualified men serve faithfully in these offices, congregations gladly follow. In many cases, they follow them and journey together into new, vibrant, unified life in their church.

Chapter 7

MEMBERSHIP
To whom am I accountable?

UPON arriving as senior pastor of my own church revitalization effort, I was troubled immediately about two things. First, were the 800 or more members on the membership roll with forty attending on a good Sunday morning. Second, was the absence of any kind of process where members are taken into membership. Not only was this true in the church I pastored, but it has been a consistent mark in virtually every dying church I have worked with in a revitalization process.

The common elephant in many Southern Baptist Church committee rooms when assessing what's not right in the church is the inflated membership numbers compared to the amount of members who actually attend on Sunday. How membership is viewed in a local church can speak volumes to its health. This area revolves around the question, 'To whom am I accountable?' A church must honestly confront what these inflated membership numbers mean in order to arrive at a patient and thoughtful solution.

The solution to some degree will revolve around a conviction that being a member of a local church is essential in the life of any Christian. Then, is the conviction that membership has to matter to the members of a local church. Meaningful membership reminds Christians that walking with Jesus in our daily life must not be done alone. We need each other. We need to be responsible for one another. Membership provides the structure for this community life that is found all throughout the New Testament. A clear understanding of how the members of a church are called to relate to one another is a key in preparing them to move forward and find new life. There are four main areas where members of a church who make a covenant with one another are to relate to each other out of love for one another and hold each other accountable:

- *Sin*

One of the most important and clearly biblical roles that members play is holding each other accountable for how they live their life and carry the name of Jesus. This is seen in several passages where members are to confront unrepentant sin in the lives of each other. In Matthew 18:15-18 Jesus describes in detail a four-step process that a Christian takes with another Christian who has sinned against him that ends with the exclusion of the offending member by 'the church' if no resolution is found. In 1 Corinthians 5:2 Paul demands that the members of the Corinthian church remove those in the church who are committing gross sexual immorality. Paul encourages the church in Thessalonica to confront those who were taking advantage of the generosity of the church (2 Thess. 3:6-15). Members of a local church are to watch their own life as well as the lives of each other, for the name of Christ and the purity of His church are at stake.

- *Suffering*

The Christian life was never designed to be lived alone. This may show to be most powerful when we suffer. The fallen world in which we live assures us we will suffer; by God's design we have each other in order that we might not suffer lonely and alone. This reality of a Christian's suffering is clear all throughout the Bible, but how we suffer together is most clearly and concisely stated in Paul's letter to the church in Galatia. Paul addresses the whole church and writes these words, 'Bear one another's burdens' (Gal. 6:2). Christians are called not just to suffer alongside one another; the command is that we actually take on each other's burdens like they were our own. This mutual burden-bearing best takes place within the covenant community of a local church. We are called to suffer together and are to assure each other we will not suffer alone.

- *Discouragement*

This fallen world also brings with it trials, pain, and struggles that inevitably produce discouragement. While some believers are more prone to discouragement, all will face it. This is why Paul instructed the faithful church in Thessalonica to, 'admonish the unruly, encourage the fainthearted, help the weak, be patient with everyone' (1 Thess. 5:14). Christians who have made a commitment to walk through life together are not to do so simply when things are good and encouraging. In fact, the powerful witness of Christians living life together is when they accept each other where they are, love each other, embrace the brokenness that exists in our lives, and encourage and help those who are weak and discouraged.

- *Affirmation*

The members of a congregation that live life together are in the best and most credible position to affirm the true, genuine faith of someone. We are not God. We are only human. We cannot ultimately know someone's heart and know whether they belong to Christ. But we have been given many different ways in the New Testament to assess the life of someone who professes to follow Jesus. The Apostles give examples of not just the pastors affirming the faith of someone, but the power in the congregation as a whole doing so.

There are two strong indications of this reality, both of which revolve around the restoration of a brother once confronted in unrepentant sin. The first example is when Paul writes to the church in Galatia and instructs them, 'Brethren, even if anyone is caught in any trespass, you who are spiritual, restore such a one in a spirit of gentleness; each one looking to yourself, so that you too will not be tempted' (Gal. 6:1). The affirmation of an individual's repentance becomes a means of accountability for the one restored as well as those who restore.

The second example comes in 2 Corinthians 2 where Paul writes to the Corinthian church. Apparently, a member of the church was put out of the church because of unrepentant sin, but now Paul wants the members to affirm him back into the fellowship. Notice the reason: 'Sufficient for such a one is this punishment which was inflicted by the majority, so that on the contrary you should rather forgive and comfort him, otherwise such a one might be overwhelmed by excessive sorrow. Wherefore, I urge you to reaffirm your love for him' (vv. 6-8). It is the members of the Corinthian Church in all their struggles and immaturities to whom Paul gives the power to restore and reaffirm their love for this one who had once been disciplined. In both cases, the individual members of the church are given the responsibility and authority to restore in a spirit of gentleness and love.

Therefore, because of all that is at stake in the individual lives of the members and the name of Christ they each carry, membership must matter in a local church. What is too common among churches that need revitalization is that the meaning of membership is gradually lost as the backbone in the life of the church. For the sake of managing growing numbers, a process of assessing potential members falls by the wayside. But when the church begins to decline, that process that has been lost is no longer in place to hold one another accountable. Unresolved conflicts fester into divisions and the members of the church stop bearing burdens with each other and making efforts to lift the downcast among them. As the church begins to panic at their dwindling numbers throughout the decades, they begin to take any warm, willing bodies into membership with no accountability or expectation. Sins of the members continue to be overlooked, eventually evolving into no godly standard of living whatsoever. In fact a common mark in dying, divided churches is a feeling of entitlement to privacy that prevents being involved in each other's lives where we can transparently engage one another as God designed.

Christians need each other. We need others to bear our burdens, weep together, suffer with us, encourage and help one another when weak and despairing. We need others to walk through life together and love us just as we are. God's design for this biblical model is meant to be carried out in the context of a local church. A dying, divided church cannot find new life and unity without assessing its membership. Membership provides the means to carry out these clear and powerful commands to Christ's local churches orchestrated to reflect God's design and glory.

CHAPTER 8

UNITY

Who is my brother?

THERE remains a growing trend to perpetuate local churches with only one generation present. On the one hand, there exist the old, historical, local churches, but hard times and steady decline have left these once vibrant churches on the edge of closing. These churches typically contain long-time faithful members who are of the older generation. On the other hand, there is the rapidly growing church planting movement where young, zealous church planters are ready to set the world on fire for Jesus; name a city, study the type of young, unchurched professionals who live there, then set out to plant a church there. These churches often times are multi-cultural, and they are almost always of the younger generation.

In an amazing irony, it seems the most zealous, faithful, and hard-working of those in the older and younger generations in these churches agree on something—that one of their biggest hindrances in the growth and ministry of the local church is the other—each is convinced they don't need the other. For a church to possess true spiritual life, there must be a unifying of the generations. Not just the unifying of generations, but also gender, race, and socio-ethnic diversities should exist in every local church to some degree (Titus 2:1-10). As a result, a very important question that must be asked in preparation for revitalization is, Who is my brother or my sister? Regardless of how different he or she is from me, Will I love this person like he is my brother or sister in Christ?

This chapter addresses the fourth area that needs to be evaluated if a church desires revitalization—*unity*. As stated earlier, hostile division among church members can kill a church and suck the life out of a church about as well as anything. When you find a local church needing revitalization, you will too often find one generation, one race, or one kind of socio-economic class. The biblical paradigm for church health is not about numbers and money despite the fact that many make it out to be. Rather, it is about a group of people who love Jesus, love each other, and are very different from the other. Spiritual life and health comes in the unity of diversity. The New Testament assumes diversity in the local church, and the unifying of people different than each other displays the power of the gospel. The clearest example of this biblical reality is captured when Paul wrote to Titus on how these new churches being started in Crete are to look:

> [1]But as for you, speak the things which are fitting for sound doctrine. [2]Older men are to be temperate, dignified, sensible, sound in faith, in love, in perseverance. [3]Older women likewise are to be reverent in their behavior, not malicious gossips nor enslaved to much wine, teaching what is good, [4]so that they may encourage the young women to love their husbands, to love their children, [5]to be sensible, pure, workers at home, kind, being subject to their own husbands, so that the word of God will not be dishonored.

⁶Likewise urge the young men to be sensible; ⁷in all things show yourself to be an example of good deeds, with purity in doctrine, dignified, ⁸sound in speech which is beyond reproach, so that the opponent will be put to shame, having nothing bad to say about us. ⁹Urge bondslaves to be subject to their own masters in everything, to be well-pleasing, not argumentative, ¹⁰not pilfering, but showing all good faith so that they will adorn the doctrine of God our Savior in every respect.

¹¹For the grace of God has appeared, bringing salvation to all men, ¹²instructing us to deny ungodliness and worldly desires and to live sensibly, righteously and godly in the present age, ¹³looking for the blessed hope and the appearing of the glory of our great God and Savior, Christ Jesus, ¹⁴who gave Himself for us to redeem us from every lawless deed, and to purify for Himself a people for His own possession, zealous for good deeds. ¹⁵These things speak and exhort and reprove with all authority. Let no one disregard you. (Titus 2:1-15)

Paul's central message in the letter to Titus is that the gospel of Jesus Christ transforms minds and hearts, and thus changes how we live. Paul's blueprint to establish healthy churches first identifies those qualified to lead the church (pastors/elders, 1:5-9), then exposes the false teachers in their midst, the gospel imposters who 'profess to know God, but deny Him by their deeds' (1:16).

Then we come to chapter 2 where Paul instructs Titus to teach followers of Jesus to live out the gospel. Paul gives a counter-cultural and even counter-intuitive design of older, younger, ethnically diverse believers loving one another, displaying the gospel to the world through affectionate, diverse, multi-generational, multi-ethnic relationships in the church. Implied in this passage is God's clear design of what a healthy local church full of gospel life looks like:

God's design for the local church is a diverse,
multi-generational, multi-ethnic local church.

This design is specifically highlighted in Titus 2 in the two-fold division of this chapter. Verses 1-10 describe the different kinds of people assumed to be in these new churches in Crete, their roles and how they display the gospel in the local church. Verses 11-15 demonstrate what that gospel is that transforms and empowers these different groups to be united. It is important to note that Paul is not instructing different churches; each of these kinds of people is represented in each of these newer local churches that Titus is establishing.

Within this chapter, Paul addresses three different categories of people that cover the gamut of diversity to create this design that is to be present in every local church. In the unity of these different groups of people the transforming power of the gospel is displayed.

Diversity on display

1) Old and young
Paul instructs Titus that the older (vv. 2-3) are to teach and train the younger (vv. 4-8). It is directly said of the older women (v. 4), and implied by the common godly character of older and younger men. It should not be overlooked that even Paul is modeling this design through his instruction and pastoral mentoring of Titus in this letter.

2) Men and Women
Paul highlights the fact that the roles of men and women are unique and distinct roles in the local church. Each group is to play their part. The instructions also vary between men and women presumably because of the sinful snares that affect men maybe more than women and vice versa.

3) Slave and Master
Bond slaves (vv. 9-10) are instructed by Paul to submit to their masters in everything in a godly manner. The closest modern equivalent to this relationship is boss and employee. However, in the first century church, there were a lot more issues present that represented a social-economic diversity, including issues of prejudice on several levels.

Given these differences, it is impossible for these different kinds of groups to love each other and be in fellowship with one another apart from the grace of God appearing and bringing salvation (v. 11). Jesus Christ came to earth, gave Himself for us on the cross, bearing the wrath of God for our sins so that He might redeem us and purify for Himself a people for His own possession, zealous for good deeds (v. 14).

What are those good deeds that display the transforming power of this gospel? It is when old and young, men and women, and even slaves and masters conduct themselves in these ways Paul has instructed (Titus 2:1-10). Through these specific and detailed instructions, Paul reveals God's design for the local church—a diverse, multi-generational, multi-ethnic local church made up of all kinds of different people who display the gospel through denying ungodliness and worldly desires and living sensibly, righteously and godly in the present age (v. 12).

Churches in need of revitalization have often times lost sight of both the need for unity and diversity. It is all too common for a church to have a difficult conflict that causes great harm to the people of the church. There may be leadership that leaves over it. Many churches exist because they split from another church over a disagreement or unnecessary conflict that was never resolved. Some churches simply lose sight that the church is to be made up of redeemed sinners purchased by the blood of Jesus who look, talk, and act differently than they do. Historically, racial tensions between black and white Christians have caused Sunday morning worship to be the most segregated hour of the week in America.

Lasting spiritual life comes through a pursuit of God's design for His church. It is when the older teach and mentor the younger; when the younger seek the older for wisdom and godly examples; when men and women embrace their unique roles with other men and women; when black, white, rich, poor, slaves, and masters unite under the reality of having been saved by the blood of Christ in the power of the gospel. Where that unity is found, life comes with it.

A turning point in the revitalization work in our church came on a Saturday morning work day. One of our young single brothers from Scotland, Mike, chose to work outside, trimming shrubs with an older couple and long-time members in the church, Howard and Mae. My first concern with this scenario was that Mike was from Scotland and has an accent that reflects it.

Mae—let's just say she's not from Scotland. She's from Kentucky! Mae has been working hard to plant trees and shrubs at our church longer than Mike has been alive. Additionally, Mike had quite a bit of experience trimming shrubs back in Scotland, so there was another legitimate concern that he may not receive well the instruction from Mae about how to do this. Mae likes to give instruction on these things. They worked all morning together and I had heard nothing.

Lunch ended. Mike and I went outside to look at the shrubs. As he showed me the fruit of his labors, Mike went on and on about how much he loved getting to work with Howard and Mae. He talked about how much he learned about the history of the church from them and what was going on when this tree was planted and that bush was placed in the ground. That was a relief, but I had yet to talk to Mae.

The next morning was Sunday. Just before the service started, Mae walks up to me with a big smile on her face and said, 'Boy, I really like that Mike! He is a good worker! I don't understand much that he says, but I like him a lot.' Do you see the unifying power of the gospel in that? Here are two people of different age, gender, social-economic class, and even nationality who could find all kinds of reasons to dislike the other. And yet they are unified because of their love for Christ and our church. With spiritual eyes they are able to look upon the other, see the value they are to one another, and embrace God's design for the local church.

So, who is my brother/sister? It is first and foremost any person who has placed their faith and trust in Jesus Christ and has been transformed by the power of the gospel. It is a sinner saved by God's grace who may be of a different generation, different race or ethnic group. It may be someone who lives on the other side of the tracks from you or speaks a different language than you. It may be your boss, or one of your lowly employees. A church that needs revitalization needs to take a hard look at this question, Who are the kinds of people who are not welcome in our church? Dying, divided churches cannot find true, lasting spiritual life if they are not willing to receive and love all those who belong to Christ. Regardless of how different someone may be from us, if they belong to Christ—they are your brother or sister. God's design is that this motley crew of God's redeemed people come under the one banner of 'Christ and Him crucified' and experience a love and fellowship that magnifies the true unifying power of the gospel.

CHAPTER 9

WORSHIP

Why do we gather together?

I SPENT the first eight years of my pastoral ministry serving in the music ministry at large churches where the music drove the church. We were taught if we wanted to reach this type of person and this age of person, we needed to do the songs they would like and do them the way they would like. What happens is that when you cater to a certain group with your music in the church, you alienate all the others. As a result, the public gathering of the church then highlights what people like to divide on, instead of what we should be unifying around. Even worse, the congregation is taught that the public gathering of the church on Sunday is about our preferences, desires, likes, and to the pragmatist—entertainment. But, the Bible gives a very different reason for gathering.

The Bible is clear that Christians are commanded to regularly gather together to worship (Heb. 10:25). But a common question that every church needs to ask, especially as they set their hands to pursue new life as a church, is this, Why do we gather? Too often the Sunday morning gathering of the local church becomes this meeting of preferences instead of the time to unify under the power of God's word for the purpose of worshiping Jesus Christ.

Songs and music styles are chosen to meet all the different musical preferences instead of being content driven and musically creative, but simple. Sermons become topics about what people want to hear, instead of simply reading and preaching God's word as the central focus of the local church when it gathers. Knowing it is the power of the Holy Spirit through the word of God that breathes life into a church, how should that inform a church about its public gathering? If a church truly believes that God's word builds the church, then it must be reflected when the church gathers for corporate worship.

This chapter addresses the fifth and final area that a church must evaluate to find spiritual life and gospel unity—*worship*. The public gathering of the church on Sunday morning is the front door and that which most visitors first observe about a church. Because of this, the morning service becomes the primary tool for the pragmatist to pull out the newest and latest tricks and gimmicks. For the purist, it can become an intentionally boring dirge, taunting all who attend to criticize the service, thereby exposing certain attenders as those who lack a desire to worship God. We are to gather as Christians to worship God with all our heart, mind, soul, and strength. If God's word by His Spirit is what breathes new life into a church, a church seeking revitalization must assure that God's word and the power of His Spirit become the central focus of the gathering. There are many ways to conduct a public worship service of God's redeemed people that is creative, powerful, and moving, while still maintaining a centrality to Scripture.

A helpful articulation of what is called the regulative principle,[1] which has been offered by authors such as Mark Dever, Paul

---

1. Briefly described, the regulative principle states that corporate worship in the local church is ordered and controlled by the specific commands of Scripture.

Alexander, and Ligon Duncan, is to preach the Bible, read the Bible, pray the Bible, sing the Bible, and see the Bible. [2] Describing Christian worship in this way allows God's authoritative and inspired word to shape the form and content of worship.

Worship Template[3]

- *Preach the word*

God has ordained the preaching of His word as the essential means for conversion. This belief was so basic for the Apostle Paul that he questioned how unbelievers would become Christians 'without someone preaching' (Rom. 10:14). God's word is profitable for the full range of Christian ministry, including teaching, reproving, correcting, and training (2 Tim. 3:16). Since God's word has this kind of usefulness, pastors must 'preach the word' (2 Tim. 4:2). The local church has always been the place for people who devote themselves to receiving the teaching of God's word (Acts 2:42).

The importance of preaching should affect the planning of worship. Local church leaders must not detract from the importance of preaching in attitude, deed, or word. Sometimes, a pastor might commend the worship accompanists with this kind of jest: 'That music was so great; I think we could all go home after that.' Another common attitude is to equate worship primarily with music, as though worship ends with the song before the sermon and resumes with the song after the sermon. However, because God's word is profitable and because preaching unleashes the profitability of God's word in the power of the Spirit, the preaching of God's word is truly the highlight of the local church's weekly gathering.

---

2. Mark Dever and Paul Alexander, *The Deliberate Church: Building Your Ministry on the Gospel* (Wheaton: Crossway 2005), pp. 77-88; Ligon Duncan, 'Does God Care How We Worship' and 'Foundations for Biblically Directed Worship,' in *Give Praise to God: A Vision for Reforming Worship* (Phillipsburg: P&R Publishing 2003), pp. 17-73.

3. This worship template is developed in greater detail in my book I wrote with Jason Adkins, *Gather God's People: Understand, Plan, and Lead Worship in the Local Church* (Grand Rapids: Zondervan 2015).

- *Read the word*

In too many churches, the sermon provides the only moments when God's people hear God's word. However, the New Testament, and specifically the Apostle Paul, envisions God's word audibly present throughout Christian worship. Paul commands his protégé, Timothy, to devote himself to the 'public reading of Scripture' (1 Tim. 4:13). Interestingly, he gave the command for his letters to receive a similar public audience (Col. 4:16; 1 Thess. 5:27). Since God's word is profitable (2 Tim. 3:16), then the reading of Spirit-inspired scripture from both the Old and New Testaments benefits God's people.

Church leaders should, therefore, incorporate the public reading of God's word in their worship gatherings. The public reading of Scripture can play several roles in the worship service. Through a call to worship, a church leader can read God's word near the beginning of a service to elicit the attention and participation of worshipers. The Psalms and other praise-oriented passages—for example, the songs of Hannah (1 Sam. 2:1-10), Mary (Luke 1:46-55), and heavenly hosts (Rev. 5:9-14; 15:3-4)—exemplify the attitudes, emotions, and thoughts that Christians should have in worship. An appropriate opening passage also introduces key themes that will reoccur throughout the time of worship. Other passages related to the sermon text or certain songs can also be read throughout the service, giving valuable time to the public reading of Scripture.

- *Pray the word*

Corporate prayer finds both its charge and content in God's word. The commands and examples of Scripture give believers a full agenda for prayer, and the public gathering is an apt time and place for practicing the discipline of prayer. Basic human needs, such as the provision of food (Matt. 6:11) and good health (3 John 2), should be matters of prayer. Christians pray for the conversion and salvation of others (Rom. 10:1). Other believers and their growth in godliness is a high priority for prayer, as the Apostle Paul shows when he prays for Christians' unity (Rom. 15:5-6); hope, joy, and peace (15:13); experience of grace (1 Cor. 16:23); wisdom, revelation, and knowledge (Eph. 1:16-17); increased love and spiritual fruit

(Phil. 1:9-11); and endurance and patience (Col. 1:11-12). When fellow believers suffer crises, such as threatening illnesses, Christians pray for them (James 5:14-15). God's people confess their sins to each other (James 5:16) and, through prayer, to God (Dan. 9:4-5).

Pastors greatly need the prayers of those in their charge and of likeminded believers in other congregations. The Apostle Paul's frequent prayer requests are good guides in praying for gospel ministers. Christians should pray for pastors to have boldness in declaring the gospel (Eph. 6:18-19), opportunities to declare Christ (Col. 4:2), favorable reception of their messages (2 Thess. 3:1), and deliverance from persecutors (2 Thess. 3:2). Christians are admonished to pray for authorities, specifically that their leadership will allow Christians to live lives that are 'peaceful and quiet' (1 Tim. 2:1-2). The best way to pray God's word is to allow Scripture to inform the content and zeal of those public prayers.

- *Sing the word*

As it does with prayer, Scripture insists upon and informs congregational singing. Church leaders can look to a variety of sources for guidance on their worship ministries—blogs, conferences, magazines, and popular contemporary Christian music. Before leaders consider the advice of these sources, they need a framework for the Bible's instructions on congregational singing. All of a church's decisions on song selection and styles should pass through this filter. Biblical faithfulness is the single most important criterion for church leaders to consider.

A seminal text on congregational singing is Ephesians 5:19. This admonishment was clearly an important part of Paul's vision for the local church because he repeats the same encouragement to the church at Colossae (Col. 3:16). In the context of Ephesians 5, Paul's instruction regarding congregational singing fills out his charge to the Ephesians that they should live wisely and watch their walk (Eph. 5:15). Specifically, verse 19 gives detail to the command 'be filled with the Spirit' (Eph. 5:18). Paul envisions believers 'addressing one another in psalms and hymns and spiritual songs, singing and making melody to the Lord with your heart' (Eph. 5:19 ESV). Here is a wise question to ask to determine if style or content drive the music and singing of a church: 'Do people leave a service at your church talking more about how the music was done, or what wonderful truth you sang about?'

- *See the word*

The ordinances of baptism and the Lord's Supper are important elements of Christian worship. These two practices were instituted under the divine authority of Jesus Christ. The Christian ordinance of baptism is part of the enduring mission of the church (Matt. 28:19). After unbelievers are converted to Christ, they receive the ordinance of baptism from a local congregation of believers by being submerged in water and raised out of it. Baptism is deeply symbolic of conversion, salvation, and union with Christ (Rom. 6:1-4). Thus, the practice depicts to all who see it that sinful humans can receive the benefits of Christ's death and anticipate the glory of a resurrection that is like Christ's own.

Similarly, Jesus Christ instituted the Lord's Supper and expected that Christians would repeat the practice throughout the ages (1 Cor. 11:23-26). Christians participate in the Lord's Supper by eating bread and drinking from a cup. These elements are wonderfully symbolic of Christ's death for sins. Just as Christ broke the bread and distributed it at the first Lord's Supper, so He also freely gave of His body for the benefit of those who believe on the cross. As one pours a drink into his mouth from a cup, so also Christ poured out His blood to achieve the forgiveness of sins. When congregations partake of the Lord's Supper, they strikingly 'proclaim the Lord's death' (1 Cor. 11:26). A centrality to God's word in the public gathering will not only determine the regular practices of these ordinances, but assure a right administration of them in a way that exalts Jesus and His saving benefits.

Many dying, divided churches have forgotten the reason Christians gather for worship. They lose confidence in God's word being what brings life while experiencing the pressure of needing to increase their attendance, and as a result fall into pragmatism, or even worse—apostasy. There is a lie that music has to be cool, hip, and contemporary to attract the younger generation who, in the eyes of many, represent new life. This falsehood appeals to many churches who are older, declining, and desperate to stop the bleeding. Movie clips, secular music, funny skits, and a sloppy administration of the ordinances move the public gathering of a church, which is intended to worship Christ, into a consumeristic sideshow. Consequently, when Christ is not lifted up, the gospel is not proclaimed, and God's word is not the central focus when the church gathers—true lasting spiritual life will not be found.

Why do Christians gather for worship? The first reason is to obey God's command (Heb. 10:25). A church can gather together several times a week, but if we don't make much of Jesus and make God's word central in the content of those gatherings, we no longer gather in the name of Christ and for His glory. For only when Christ and His word are lifted up does a church bring Him glory and ultimately call upon His life-giving power to awaken the dead in their midst.

Section III:
Church Revitalization – Done

CHAPTER 10

HISTORY AND BACKGROUND

WHEN I first shared the story of my first ten years in church revitalization, I found it to be unexpectedly difficult. I relived some very painful memories, reminders of bad decisions with many unpleasant consequences, not least of which is the toll they took on my family that is still palpable. These old wounds remind me of what wounded sheep will do if they have been harmed deeply by previous shepherds.

As painful as these recollections may be, I feel compelled to share them in the hope they serve other pastors, encouraging trust that God is at work and that pastors struggling in the trench work of ministry would remain steadfast. It is also my aim to allow my story to act as a real-life example of what is advocated in this book. The principles, insights, and convictions articulated in this work do not come from abstract theories, but from real-life blood, sweat, and tears living in the trenches of this noble work of church revitalization.

My intent in telling my story of revitalization is to recount a history of the first ten years of my ministry at Auburndale Baptist Church, followed by five invaluable lessons God taught me through these experiences in the hope that pastors will be able to incorporate them into their own ministry and church situation. I want us to consider Hebrews 13:17 as a banner over this account, for when I am asked why I stayed as I walked through these hard years, I always come back to this sobering responsibility to pastors:

> Obey your leaders and submit to them, for they keep watch over your souls *as those who will give an account*. Let them do this with joy and not grief, for this would be unprofitable for you. (Heb. 13:17, italics added)

I came to Auburndale Baptist Church in September 2003 knowing this church had a reputation of chewing up and spitting out pastors. My wife knew it too, which is why she did not want to go. This church had been in decline for over three decades with pastors staying between one to three years on average, four years being the longest stay since 1972. The church began in 1938 as a neighborhood Bible study. This church eventually became one of the largest congregations in the city of Louisville in the 1950s and 1960s, growing large under the tenure of one pastor who stayed twenty years. When he retired in 1972, the church began its slow, steady decline immediately with the next pastor.

In the early 1980s, the current pastor of the church caused a stir over non-essential issues that led to a church-wide vote on whether he should stay as pastor. The perfectly even split vote of 150 to 150 is a rarity in congregational churches. If this ever happens in a member's meeting (i.e. business meeting), the tie is to be decided by a vote of the moderator. He refused to vote. This caused the pastor to leave the church, take half of the congregation with him, and start another church two blocks away. I have been told by many who were in that room that day of the heartbreak and discouragement that resulted. Friends rejected each other. Families split in this decision, some staying and some leaving. In 1983 when the smoke cleared,

Auburndale Baptist Church consisted of 150 wounded members who had been abandoned by their shepherd and were now without a pastor.

Over the next twenty years the church endured numerous short pastorates, steady decline, and hard times. I arrived on the heels of that to find a hurting, wounded, and divided congregation of approximately forty elderly people. The church was about two to three years from closing its doors if nothing changed. I saw the financial numbers through the interview process, but could not assess until I arrived how desperate the church finances were, which was most painfully realized when I saw they hired me at a salary that could not be sustained longer than six months. The church was so rife with disunity that even the surrounding community recognized it, earning the church the appalling reputation it rightly deserved. I was often reminded that I would be the church's last pastor.

Thankfully, I had very wise mentors who taught me well. I came with two commitments that I learned from them. First, I must faithfully preach the word, sacrificially love the people, and not change anything for a while. Second, regardless of what happens, stay ten years. I had come to a deep conviction that the word of God was enough to breathe life into a church, unify it, and build it—even an existing church that appeared to have little to no life left in it. One precious gift the Lord gave us was another family, close friends of ours, who came to the church with us. From day one as senior pastor of this struggling church my friend served as my associate pastor for the first four years. He said he was coming to get ministry experience as he was considering vocational pastoral ministry. He later admitted he and his wife came to care for us in what they expected to be a rough place. As you are about to read, they were right.

The best way to approach this history is in five year divisions. The first five years were brutal and are captured in the next chapter. Thankfully, in year six the ship turned, which will be the chapter to follow. Then, I would like to highlight five lessons I learned in this painful, but rewarding journey of revitalization. I would also like to add an important note here in regard to my wife before you experience *our story*. Local church ministry is hard for a pastor, but there is one harder place to experience difficulty, attacks, and slander in pastoral ministry—the place of the pastor's wife. This is our story as she endured all these struggles and attacks by my side and experienced the same pain and hurt I did—probably more so. Don't miss the fact that the hero in a pastor remaining steadfast in a hostile church situation is often not the pastor, but his resilient, supportive, and faithful wife. This was, without a doubt, true for us and our story.

One final disclaimer: This story needs to be read realizing two things: The sheep of this church had been severely wounded for decades by shepherds. The cynical distrust of the sheep towards the next shepherd that I experienced should not be surprising. It was a broken, hurting church. However, when I came, this church hired a pastor that was just as broken. These ten years were a journey for my wife and me, who needed to grow, learn, and find spiritual health just as this church did. Therefore, read this story as a journey of redemption and new life for not just this broken church that needed revitalization, but for the broken pastor they hired who needed to learn how to experience and trust in God's grace and power.

CHAPTER 11

THE STORM
The first five years

A LL the rumors we had heard about Auburndale's appetite for
pastors proved to be true. No honeymoon period for me.
There were three different movements to get me fired in the first
five years at the church. Sadly, these have become the markers
for those first five years, mainly because the issues that stirred
this pot of hostility exposed the problems and issues that needed
to be addressed if the church was to move out of the decades of
destructive patterns and move to a better, more healthy place. The
issues surrounding these attempted firings will look strangely
familiar to you as they represent some of the key issues this book
advocates.

Firing Effort One: Authority

I faced this attempt after just three short months as the *senior pastor* of the church. No honeymoon period for me. Three months was enough time to realize the church had hired me at a salary they could not pay me for more than six months. But more importantly, this was plenty of time to infuriate the part-time music minister I had inherited. He boasted when I got there that he was responsible for getting rid of the previous pastor and that he could do the same with me. We made a valiant effort to befriend him and invite him on board with our vision, but realized that was not happening when we got word of him approaching visitors on Sunday morning after the service telling them that I was crazy and they should not come here.

When we confronted him about this, he responded in a violent rage and declared war against me. He let me know that he was going to get rid of me as he had done with the previous pastor. We quickly received word he was slandering me to the church and trying to mount a support group in order to call a business meeting for the purpose of voting to remove me. I called him to confirm these rumors, which he did. As it was clear we probably were not going to work well together, I then asked him to resign. I told him I would give him the chance to resign and leave peacefully, stating that the church had gone through enough already and further conflict would only make things worse. My proposal was met with threats and attacks, bringing me to the realization he was not going to back down.

In that instant, I had an insight that felt like it came from the Holy Spirit. To be honest, I am still not sure about it. Some may be horrified by my actions. In that moment of extreme emotional duress, I realized I had a point of leverage with him that I could use with the intent of getting him to leave the church peacefully without causing further damage among the congregation. With words admittedly prejudiced by my own anger I said to him,

> OK, you may take me on and win. You may call for and win
> a vote to remove me and I cannot do anything about it. But,
> if you choose to go this way, and you lose, I promise you,

I will do everything in my power to make sure you never,
ever get another ministry job in your life.

The phone was silent. At length I heard, 'You wouldn't do that.'
With frightening intensity I responded, 'Just try me.' He would
soon be graduating from seminary and he knew that every church
would call me for a reference since I pastored the only church he had
ever served. I agreed not to hinder his future ministry if he agreed
to leave peacefully, giving him three days to respond to my request
for his peaceful resignation.

Three days came and went. I heard nothing. Some church
members, my wife included, feared for my safety as this man had
a history of violent outbursts in church. Now it was Sunday, the
deadline having come and gone. There are few feelings like showing
up at church with the expectation of being attacked and possibly
even an attempted vote to call for your dismissal. The service
happened. I preached. All was well. Then, I went down to the front
of the pulpit to administer the Lord's Supper. As I walked down,
the music minister walked up to the pulpit, leaned down at me and
said, 'Brian, I've got something to say.' Startled by this inappropriate
request, I told him, 'I'm doing the Lord's Supper; it's going to
have to wait.' Distracted does not begin to capture my mood as I
administered the Lord's Supper.

Afterward, I felt this crazy, but peaceful impulse to allow him
to speak. Because he had not gotten back to me I had no idea what
he would say. Trusting in the Lord in that moment, I stood by as
he stood up at the end of the service and peacefully resigned. He
approached me after the room had cleared out and several people
had spoken with him. He stood there visibly shaking and said, 'You
better do what you said you would do.' I said, 'You have my word.' I
feel I have honored that word for over a decade now.

To this day, I do not know how much of that encounter honored
Jesus, and how much saddened Him. I still look back and feel
unsettled in the way I handled it. At the same time, I do not know
what other option I had at the time. In God's kind providence, a
month before this conflict and resignation of the music minister,
a young man from the seminary came to check out the church

and for some strange reason stayed. To this day, he is one of the most musically gifted and theologically sound men I know. He was hired to replace the man who resigned and faithfully served for the next four years as our music leader. To add to the strange providences of the Lord, he had the exact same first and last name as the former guy.

Firing Effort Two: Membership

I was able to keep myself out of trouble for the next year to some degree because there had been more people join the church in the first year than had the previous ten years. I do not care how much your deacons dislike you, deacons in a Southern Baptist church will overlook a lot when the church numerically grows. However, in the middle of year two, even numeric growth could not protect me from the can of worms I opened when I noted that we had forty to fifty people attending and over 600 people on the membership rolls.

I realized I had touched a nerve during a discussion of the issue in a deacons' meeting. One of the quiet deacons who rarely said much pointed his finger in my face during this conversation and said, 'Pastor, your honeymoon is over.' The following deacons' meeting was held while I was on vacation in Minnesota visiting my wife's family. I can still remember where I was standing in my wife's uncle's field in rural Minnesota. It was the only place I could find a cell signal. In the middle of that pasture I heard my associate pastor report that the deacons tried to convince him to turn against me and lead a charge behind my back to get me fired. If he agreed they would make him the pastor once I was gone. He refused.

Two things came as a result of his refusal. First, my trust in this man grew enormously. Second, my desire and willingness ever to leave town on vacation vanished. To this day I have an incredible amount of vacation built up because of my reluctance to leave town in these early years. The slow conversations about what an accurate membership looks like and why that was important continued. Although I dodged another bullet, it was at this moment that the church bank account hit zero. I was continually looking for side work during this time, not knowing if I would be paid from week to week.

Firing Effort Three: Leadership

I survived another eighteen months and the Lord was continuing to show evidence he was at work in the midst of the turmoil. But the wheels really came off in between years four and five. Older long term members continued to pass away; some of them were encouraging supporters my entire ministry there, others not so much. During this same period the church continued to grow numerically, predominantly with younger folk in their twenties and thirties desiring to come to the kind of church we had said we wanted to see at Auburndale Baptist Church. Some new arrivals were seminary students. Some were random folk the Lord was sovereignly bringing at just the right time.

Although this was encouraging to me, it was not for those who had held a stranglehold on the church for decades. By year four they came to the realization that they were outnumbered in the active church membership. That would normally be a good thing, but in a congregational church where the church membership votes on the weightier decisions of congregational life, that meant the newer folk now had the power to make decisions. Once the old regime realized this, it really got ugly. Certain leaders in the church began to drive by the church a few times a day, keeping a journal of when my car was there or not to bring charges against me that I was not working.

Eighty percent of the search committee that hired me had left the church angry, slandering me on their way out over different issues. Fifteen percent of the congregation—both newer and older members—left in this year. It got so bad during this time that only I and my associate had keys to my office, as there were threats that I would be set up. The man leading the charge against me was a leader in the church. It was rumored that he had previously planted something that got a staff member fired twenty years earlier. It was during this time that my associate who had cared for me and protected me through all this left to accept a full time pastorate in North Carolina.

In the middle of a Wednesday evening Bible Study I was teaching, a deacon's wife stood up and verbally attacked me. She said such horrible things about me that it sent church members running out of the room sobbing. This was particularly difficult for my wife. Thankfully, she was working in the nursery that evening. Not so thankfully, she was met by hysterical women coming to get their children and greeting her with the words, 'You are not going to believe what happened and what was said to your husband!' At this point my wife was just making sure no one pulled a gun on me in light of the way people were responding.

There were many issues at play during this time that stirred up everyone, but the main issue was that I was trying to move to a plurality of pastors. I spent eighteen months teaching through First Timothy without once saying we should do this. All I did was teach, trying to lay the foundation for a future implementation based on the authority of God's word. But the moment I began to talk about what this would look like and why, it was like gasoline on the fire. My goal of moving to a plurality of pastors was rooted in my desire to share my authority with other qualified men so that the church would be cared for even better. Unfortunately, it was seen by some as me trying to take more authority for myself. It was during this situation that I met the director of our local association of Baptist churches. A handful of my church members went to him to tell them I was teaching some heresy they had never heard of, trying to make the church Presbyterian.

The low moment came at the funeral of a beloved church member. I received word that an impromptu meeting had been called by several church members in the kitchen of the funeral home during the visitation. Their plan was simple: during the next church business meeting they wanted to vote down the forthcoming motion on a plurality of pastors and then hastily vote to remove me. That may seem improbable given what I have already said about the old regime now being in the minority. But those familiar with the negative aspects of congregational church life gone awry will not be surprised by what unfolded. This church business meeting was mysteriously attended by 'members' who had not been to church in years. What they did not realize was that I had already told the leader of the opposition group that I was not going to put it forward for a vote, for I realized it was about to split the church.

I remember my conversation with this man like it was yesterday. I said to him, 'I have the votes for this motion. You know it and I know it. But, I am not putting it forward. I am withdrawing the motion as I feel it will harm the church. But, you are harming the church also, so if I remove the motion, will you agree to back off?' He agreed. I also remember something very puzzling that happened: he seemed surprised and even a little grateful. When the smoke cleared, fifteen percent of the church was gone, most of the committee that hired me was gone, the church was broke, and I felt like the last eighteen months of work went up in flames when I pulled that motion off the table. I was done—almost.

Anytime I thought of leaving I was moved to stay for two reasons. First, we had been through so much that I did not believe God would take us through these trials only to then abandon us. He had more planned. Second, I was haunted by Hebrews 13:17. I was haunted by the reality that I would one day give an account for the souls of not just those sheep who loved and supported me, but those who did not and even tried to fire me. Just because they did not like me or my decisions as a pastor did not mean they were wolves. So I stayed. By God's grace, some of them stayed too. In God's kind providence, the ship then began to turn.

CHAPTER 12

THE SHIP TURNS
The next five years

IN the kind mysterious providence of God, when the smoke cleared from this implosion, I looked up to discover that the ship had started to turn. Almost like clockwork as we entered into the sixth year, significant issues began to change. After the smoke cleared from the mass exodus, some of the most significant families in our church today showed up in the next year—three of the men now serve as pastors with me.

I made some needed adjustments in my preaching where I became more open, vulnerable, and broken before my people—that has been life-giving to them. We began to reach the community, particularly international refugees living around the church. The horrible reputation that the church carried for the last twenty-five years began to change as we became more visible to those around us. There are many other things I could share indicating that change was around the corner. However, there were two significant events that took place in the next two years that stand above the others.

First, a plurality of pastors was affirmed by the church. When I pulled the motion off the table, I felt like I had failed. So I spent the next six months going to certain people's homes to ask them why they were so opposed to this idea. A game changing insight came. The entire time I was proposing to move to a plurality of pastors I had been using the phrase 'plurality of elders'. While that is the more common way of referring to the concept in many circles, the term 'elders' had fallen into disuse among Southern Baptist churches during the twentieth century.[1] These long-time Southern Baptist church members did not know what an elder was. No matter how much I taught that a pastor and elder were the same thing, my older members did not understand what an elder was. But they knew what a pastor was. I put the same motion forward that was going to split the church nine months earlier and just changed the language of elder to pastor, and it passed unanimously. That evening three men in our church were affirmed as 'pastors'. In my estimation, that has proven to be the most important decision I have made at the church.

Second, we purged our membership rolls. The whole church spent three years slowly and methodically trying to contact the list of 600 plus names of people on our membership rolls. After that long and tedious process, the pastors put forward 485 names to be voted off the membership rolls in one members' meeting. This motion also passed without a single 'no' vote. This points to the next most important decision I made and that was to establish way back in year one what it meant to become a member by adjusting the church covenant. From that time forward every incoming member understood and agreed to the definition and responsibilities of covenant membership. As a result, by year seven there was a clear distinction between those who were members of the church and those who were not, a crucial element to a healthy congregational church.

---

1. This phenomenon is witnessed by the shift in language between the 1925 and 1963 editions of the SBC statement of faith, the Baptist Faith and Message.

In a kind providence that only a gracious God can provide, what I thought was my biggest failure became one of my most fruitful decisions. When I did not press that vote and pulled it off the table even though I had the votes, the older members who up to that point had viewed me as merely one more pastor in a series of pastors out for themselves, saw for the first time that I really cared more about the church than my agenda. That was a new day in my relationships with those folks. Walls began to come down. God has given me so many sweet moments with them since. Some I have walked to the grave holding their hand because they wanted me there. Others are still at the church and warmly greet me and have even become some of my greatest advocates and supporters.

The clear divide between old and young began to close when I called on the younger members to pursue the older members. I reminded them that though Titus chapter two advocates the older mentoring the younger, our older members felt like outsiders. If we sought them out in order to love them, they would respond favorably. That is exactly what the younger crowd did and the older folk felt loved by them and it brought the generations together in a special way. A sign of health I still notice is when a single, male college student gets up at the beginning of the service to go sit with the elderly widow sitting by herself where she used to sit with her husband. Those are the little things that bring me great joy and remind me the ship had indeed turned.

I would like to tell you that year six inaugurated a sustained period of smooth sailing. But since then we have walked through miscarriages, cancer, the sudden death of a beloved young deacon, beloved church members moving away, church members unsure where their daily bread will come next week, church discipline over husbands abusing and abandoning their families, tensions between certain leaders, and many other reminders that the church is for the sick and that we still live in a fallen world. We are far from a perfect church, but without a doubt we have reached a place where by the grace and power of God we are a different church at a different place.

As I continue to pastor this church into the next decade, I am reminded that it is good to celebrate that our church is a different, more healthy church than before. Much of the life and unity that a church seeks in revitalization has been experienced and accomplished. And yet, the work is never completed. In fact, as a revitalization pastor who stayed long enough to experience this new life, there is a haunting reality that I have also stayed long enough to see my failures, weaknesses, and lack of leadership on display in our church. I have often said most pastors don't stay ten years because it is at that point where they can no longer blame the previous pastors for the problems and weaknesses in the church. The ship turned, but pastors who experience new life in a congregation must be self-aware and wise so that we don't miss how we have harmed the church in the process and created fresh struggles that need to be addressed. It is in this growing awareness in my own life that I share these five lessons learned that reflected my need to grow—and continue to grow today.

CHAPTER 13

IMPORTANT LESSONS LEARNED

MY first decade of church revitalization held many great joys. But it was also punctuated by periods of great pain. It is clearer to me now more than ever that the Lord was leading me all along the way, sometimes through joy, sometimes through pain, but nevertheless leading me. Growing turmoil in my soul exposed some dark areas that were crushing me and took its toll on others and me as I walked through these painful years. My soul was slowly being crushed under the weight of perfectionism, fear of man, major bouts of anxiety and issues with control. It was during the final period of the first ten years that I had begun the soul work necessary to allow the gospel to deepen in my soul and begin to infiltrate these areas of my life that were dark and hidden. As a result, these lessons have become more real and sweet to me as I look back on these years. I took a broken church. But my brokenness equaled, if not surpassed the brokenness of this church. Out of my brokenness came these five important lessons:

The Epiphany of Patience

In the early years, I thought I was the patient one. I was enduring through the criticisms, judgments, and actions to remove me. I was being the bigger, more faithful person. As the years have passed, I have realized in a lot of ways more and more that it was the other way around. These long-time faithful saints wounded by previous pastors for decades were being patient with me. They were being patient with me as I grew as a preacher. The eighty-five-year-old widow who used to lecture me about my preaching in the early years turned out to be right. They were patient with me as I made rookie mistakes. They were patient with me through all the changes they did not understand or agree with and somehow with blind faith tried to trust this man who was young enough to be their grandson. Ironically, I should not be celebrated as one who endured, but one who was shown a lot of grace that I did not deserve and allowed me to stay longer.

The Sweetness of Tough Love

We all want everyone to instantly receive us and our ministries, and think those ultra-supportive church members are exactly what we want. But I have learned that to have church members hostile to you, not receive you, and make you pursue them in love is a sweeter and more rewarding relationship when you win them. I have some incredibly supportive people in our church now, but the relationships that mean the most to me are those with whom I fought in the early years, struggled to love in any way, and yet we grew and learned how to love each other. To be greeted every Sunday with a smile, hug, and warmth by the man who led the charge at year five to remove me is hard to describe and it still moves me every time. That is an evidence of God's redemptive grace every time we see each other that I do not experience when I am greeted by my greatest supporters who have always been with me.

The Discerning Perspective of Scars

God in his sovereign grace uses the worst moments in our ministries to bring gratefulness and a unique perspective in a pastor's life like nothing else when real change occurs. Because of the trials I have endured in our church, I have a perspective in decision making that few in our church now have. So when our newest seminary student is really uptight about those eight to ten members on the fringe or those family members of long time church members still on the roll, he does not remember the blood, sweat, tears, and bruises that came to remove 485 members. He does not know about the bone-chilling finger-pointing threat I received in the deacons' meeting years earlier. As I remain one of the few leaders still there who witnessed and endured this struggle, I find my perspective in decision-making is much different from theirs. God grows a unique discernment and wisdom in you through the pastoral scars of the journey you have walked. Nothing can serve a pastor so well as the wisdom wrought by scars.

The Inevitability of Suffering

If you are a pastor holding on to the hope that suffering will not come, you should find another line of work now. It is amazing the number of pastors who contact me ready to resign after about two years of ministry in one place because they finally met the adversaries the enemy had placed there in that open door of ministry. As I talk with them and we begin to talk through the discouragement and struggles, I eventually ask them, 'Did you think becoming the pastor of that church would not bring with it adversaries to come against your gospel ministry?' Ironically, in many cases it is their confrontation with adversaries against the gospel and their ministries that make them conclude it is time for the next place.

The Apostle Paul takes the opposite approach—the presence of adversaries makes him conclude he must stay longer, 'But I will remain in Ephesus until Pentecost; for a wide door for effective service has opened to me, and there are many adversaries' (1 Cor. 16:8-9). Becoming a pastor means we place our families and ourselves on the front lines of spiritual battle. Why are we continually so surprised when the enemy comes against our gospel ministry, especially in places it has been suppressed for decades? Charles Simeon said, 'Brothers we must not mind a little suffering.' It is coming brothers, but it is okay.

The Steadfastness of the Chief Shepherd

The Chief Shepherd never abandons His under-shepherds. Christ promises to never leave or forsake His sheep. We preach that regularly to our people and we should. How much more so is this true for the ones who care for His sheep? I love children in general and I would do anything if I saw a child being attacked in some way. But if someone goes after my kids—it is on! He is with you! He knows. He is near and working, even when you do not see it. That is the smiling face behind the frowning providence.[1] How could we think Jesus would not fight relentlessly for those of us who faithfully labor, suffer, and endure to care for His sheep?

Herein lies the essential lesson for all pastors laboring in the work of revitalization. Jesus is with you! He is your shield in that deacons' meeting. He is there when you are publically rebuked. He is compassionate when your mistake or failure in a decision harms the church. He is sad when His sheep attack you because they do not understand and are afraid. He is your defender when wolves in the church try to harm the sheep. The Chief Shepherd will never abandon His shepherds! He is with you and doing whatever He must to give you the grace to remain steadfast in this task of caring for souls on His behalf until He returns.

Dear brothers and fellow pastors, in light of the care of the Chief Shepherd—take heart. Remain steadfast. There are so many good purposes you do not now see that our sovereign and gracious God has for you wherever you find yourself in this journey. If you will stay the course they will become evident. It will bring a sweetness to your ministry that the newest, best, most healthy church you would pack up and leave for cannot provide. Do you have the faith to believe it? Do you trust He is indeed always with you? If you can answer 'Yes' to those questions, you can endure

---

1. This is a reference to the classic line in William Cowper's hymn, 'God Moves in a Mysterious Way'.

the greatest storm and messiest church and hold fast—because the Chief Shepherd is with you!

CONCLUSION
A final appeal

CHURCH revitalization is a good and noble work. It is fraught with challenges, dangers, trials, and difficulties, and only men who are called and gifted for the task will be able to remain steadfast in them. However, for those who lean into this calling and put their hands to the plow, there are unique joys and rewards that come with this important gospel work. My hope is this book has not only convinced you of this reality, but has given you tangible, biblical solutions as you approach this work, praying God might breathe life and unite God's people in your midst.

In conclusion, I would like to make one final appeal to those who seek to engage in this work. My final appeal is this—be a courageous pastor. What do I mean by courageous? Pastors are commonly pressured to have it all together, to have it all figured out, and therefore are assumed to be the experts to instruct everyone else on how to do life. The biblical qualification of spiritual maturity and above reproach can easily slide into this unachievable perfectionistic standard that prevents many pastors from being themselves before their people. Instead, they perform.

My final appeal is for men to step up and be a courageous pastor captured in this way: *show up as broken, weak, and needy before the church you seek to pastor and revitalize.* Do not underestimate the power of God to bring life into a church when a pastor lives a real and authentic life before God's people. The reality is that pastors are just as weak, needy, and broken as everyone else in the church. Pastors need to embrace this calling to live an honest, authentic life before their people. Let them see you struggle. Let them know you are hurting. Remind them you are not perfect and are not in control. Remind them you sin—often. The most courageous pastors are the ones who don't perform, but rest in their identity in Christ and live in the freedom of being themselves before their people. Here are two ways to help your pursuit of this type of transparent living:

Strength in weakness

The idea of strength in weakness sounds like an opposing idea. Many would say you cannot be strong and weak at the same time. But the Bible gives a very different understanding, captured most clearly in a letter Paul wrote to the Corinthians when he referred to his request of God to remove a thorn in his flesh and God responds:

> My grace is sufficient for you, for power is perfected in weakness. Most gladly, therefore, I will rather boast about my weaknesses, so that the power of Christ may dwell in me. Therefore I am well content with weaknesses, with insults, with distresses ... for Christ's sake; for when I am weak, then I am strong (2 Cor. 12:9-10).

I have a confession to make. I have always affirmed Paul's teaching here as true. But I have spent most of my life living as if strength cannot co-exist with weakness. However, I am learning this is the key to understanding how to live courageously and in the freedom of the gospel. True strength comes from Jesus living in us and that is most magnified when we are weak and needy for Him. Christ's presence is most cultivated in us when we embrace the reality of our weakness, sinfulness, brokenness, and humanity. In Christ, we find true strength, not despite our weakness, *but in our weakness*. A courageous pastor embraces his weakness and finds divine strength.

Love in brokenness
There exists a close tie between embracing our brokenness with our emotions. There is something important about our emotions we need to remember. We cannot suppress emotion, be scared of emotion—then conclude we can somehow still feel deeply. We have to embrace our brokenness. One of the ways we do that is we allow ourselves to feel emotion despite any fear that might accompany doing so. It's good to cry and feel sadness. It's good to allow yourself to feel anger. It's good to allow yourself to feel fear. It's good to allow yourself to feel hurt and frustrated. God made our emotions to be the gateway to gaze into our souls. It is through our emotions that we grow aware of the activity in our souls.

I am aware of the struggle with sin that can certainly get wrapped up in these emotions. That should not be ignored. But if we don't allow ourselves to feel these emotions deeply, we cannot feel deep joy and love. The tough, unshakable, stoic cannot love deeply. Allow yourself to feel deeply because that is the only way we are able to love deeply. Jesus felt deep anguish, anger, and joy. Paul has advocated how Christians are to love deeply and sacrificially. A courageous pastor loves deeply when he embraces his own brokenness before the Lord. A broken pastor who knows he is broken will show compassion differently than a pastor who does not acknowledge his own brokenness. One shows compassion. The other shows pity.

Churches that need revitalization don't simply need pastors. This unique work requires courageous pastors. Men who are so secure in their identity in Christ that they are able to embrace their humanity, frailty, weakness, brokenness, and failures and remember that they are just as loved and accepted by Jesus because of the gospel. This kind of pastor shows up as a compassionate pastor, a humble and teachable pastor, a wise and discerning pastor able to assess the activity of his own soul and the souls of others. Revitalization pastors don't need to be perfect or have it all together. They simply need Jesus and know they need Jesus just as badly as everyone else. It is a courageous pastor who finds his strength in his weakness and deeply loves in his brokenness that helps a dead, divided, hurting, and broken church see their need for new life and unity. May God give pastors the grace needed to serve hurting churches in this way not just for the sake of Christ's church, but also to preserve the soul of the pastor doing this noble work for God's glory.

Appendix

Church Revitalization Internship Syllabus (SBTS)

Introduction

This internship syllabus was added as a resource for this book because it captures well how I am trying to train men for pastoral ministry in a seminary context, particularly for the work of church revitalization. It contains many of the ideas developed in this book, yet condensed in the form of a two semester graduate course offered at The Southern Baptist Theological Seminary. It also includes specific resources and intentional conversations necessary for students to properly understand this work. Please use this syllabus to help you develop your own approach to train and inform others of this work of church revitalization in your unique context.

Mathena Center
For
Church Revitalization
The Southern Baptist Theological Seminary

Church Revitalization Practicum (3665X)
Course Syllabus

Course Description

This practicum will prepare aspiring pastors to provide the leadership and care needed to revitalize struggling, dying churches. The course will provide an academic foundation and practical experience in the three 'stool legs' of revitalization training:

- Pastoral Theology
- Healthy Ecclesiology
- Personal Soul Care

All three elements are required to serve and endure in a church revitalization environment. Students will meet with revitalization leaders and receive individual discipleship to help prepare for this unique work.

Course Goals

Upon successful completion of the requirements of this course, students will:

1. Understand the theological framework and practical mechanics of congregational care, and the great patience required when entering the community of a struggling congregation.

2. Investigate a framework and model for understanding a multi-year strategy needed to return a struggling congregation to health.

3. Develop a biblical understanding of the primacy of God's sovereign care in the work of revitalization ministry, demonstrated primarily through shepherding the flock (1 Pet. 5:2), prayer, and the ministry of the word (Acts 6:4).

4. Cultivate and maintain their personal and spiritual well-being through being exposed to practices that will help deepen their love relationship with Jesus and mitigate the spiritual risk intrinsic within church revitalization.

5. Be exposed to a broad range of pastors and church leaders who have worked in the area of church revitalization and successfully led struggling churches to restoration.

Textbooks

Alexander, Paul and Dever, Mark. *The Deliberate Church*. Wheaton: Crossway 2005. ISBN# 1581347383

Croft, Brian and Croft, Cara. *The Pastor's Family: Shepherding Your Family Through the Challenges of Pastoral Ministry*. Grand Rapids: Zondervan 2013. ISBN# 0310495091.

Croft, Brian. *The Pastor's Ministry: Biblical Priorities for Faithful Shepherds*. Grand Rapids: Zondervan 2015. ISBN# 0310516595

Henard, William. *Can These Bones Live?* Nashville: B&H Publishing Group 2015. ISBN# 1433683970

McClellan, Kyle. *Mea Culpa*. Great Britain: Christian Focus 2015. ISBN# 1781915296

Mohler, R. Albert Jr., ed. *A Guide to Church Revitalization*. Louisville: SBTS Press 2015. ISBN# 0990349535

Piper, John. *The Roots of Endurance*. Wheaton: Crossway 2002. ISBN# 1581348142

Reeder, Henry and Swavely, David. *From Embers to a Flame*. Phillipsburg: P&R Publishing 2004. ISBN# 0875525121

Course Requirements

1. Attendance and Participation
Because presence is crucial to the work of church revitalization, students are expected to be at all class meetings and special events.

2. Reading Report

Each required text should be read reflectively, particularly focusing on how the material relates to the work of church revitalization. Students will be required to complete four books per semester and submit a reading report.

3. Reading Roundtable & Pastoral Discussions

Students will participate in class discussions of assigned readings and other material. There will also be period 'Roundtable Discussions' with successful church revitalization pastors.

4. Journaling

Students will journal once a week, preparing about 1-2 pages of text (double spaced) each time. These journals should reflect the soul work the student is doing, and reflect on how lessons learned through the readings and discussions can be practically applied in a local church context.

5. Reflection Paper #1

During final exam week of the first semester, students will submit a 7-10 page (typed; double-spaced) reflection paper. In this paper the student will select one of the practical aspects of revitalization ministry, and consider what the student has learned considering the three 'legs' of revitalization ministry taught over the semester (Pastoral Theology, Healthy Ecclesiology, Personal Soul Care). The paper should conclude with a short description of how the student would implement this particular ministry in a revitalization context.

6. Reflection Paper #2

During final exam week of the second semester, students will turn in a 7-10 page (typed; double-spaced) reflection paper. This paper will ask the students to use journal entries to reflect on how the readings and conversations have impacted them over the course of the year. The body of the paper should address specifics within the three areas of revitalization ministry.

7. Pastoral Care Observation Opportunities

Students will have some opportunity to observe pastoral care in action (Hospital Visits, Outreach Visits, Worship Planning, etc.). Students should report on these opportunities in their journal.

8. Prayer

Because the work of a Revitalization Pastor depends so much on the care for his flock, students will be expected to pray systematically for the members of their local churches.

9. Revitalization Retreat

Students will participate in a weekend conference with a church that has gone through a successful revitalization process. This will be an interactive experience allowing the students to walk through a live 'case-study' of a church coming out of a revitalization season.

Grading

Grades will be compiled from the following components:

```
Participation in Pastoral Roundtables ......... 30%
Journaling ................................................. 10%
Reading Report ............................................ 10%
Church Directory Prayer ............................ 10%
Reflection Paper #1 ..................................... 20%
Reflection Paper #2 ..................................... 20%
```

Grading Scale

A	4.0 96-100	B	3.0 86-88	C	2.0 76-78	D	1.0 66-68
A-	3.7 93-95	B-	2.7 83-85	C-	1.7 73-75	D-	0.7 63-65
B+	3.3 89-92	C+	2.3 79-82	D+	1.3 69-72	F	0.0 0-62

WP	Withdraw Pass
WF	Withdraw Fail
I	Incomplete (no grades of incomplete will be issued for this course except in an extreme circumstance as determined by the professor)

Disclaimers

1. The Church Revitalization Practicum is a year-long course. Upon successful completion of both semesters of coursework, students will receive credit for a 3-hour elective.

2. In order to ensure full participation, any student with a disabling condition requiring special accommodations (e.g., tape recorders, special adaptive equipment, special note-taking or test-taking needs) is strongly encouraged to contact the Student Associate at the beginning of the internship.

3. During the course of the semester the professor reserves the right to modify any portion of this syllabus as may appear necessary because of events and circumstances that occur during the term.

4. All students are required to affirm their academic integrity when submitting all course work with the following statement, signed by the student (at the bottom of the title page):

> *On my honor, I have neither given nor taken improper assistance in completing this assignment.*

Course Schedule

Term 1

Introduction to Internship and Syllabus
Orientation to Mathena Model of Church Revitalization
Roundtable Discussion – *A Guide to Church Revitalization*

Roundtable Discussion – *The Pastor's Ministry*
The work of a revitalization pastor

Pastoral Interview
The rewarding, redeeming work of revitalization

Roundtable Discussion – *From Embers to a Flame*
The work of revitalization

Roundtable Discussion – *The Roots of Endurance*
Faithfulness and Survival in pastoral ministry

Pastoral Interview
A long, patient road to Faithfulness (5–10 years rule)
First Term Reading Complete

Term 2

Roundtable Discussion – *The Deliberate Church*
Ecclesiology matters

Pastoral Interview
Picking your battles wisely

Roundtable Discussion – *Mea Culpa*
Mistakes made in Church Revitalization

Pastoral Interview
Planting vs. Revitalization

Roundtable Discussion – *Can These Bones Live*
Pastoral Interview – Unsuccessful Revitalizations

Roundtable Discussion – *The Pastor's Family*
Closing reflections and evaluation

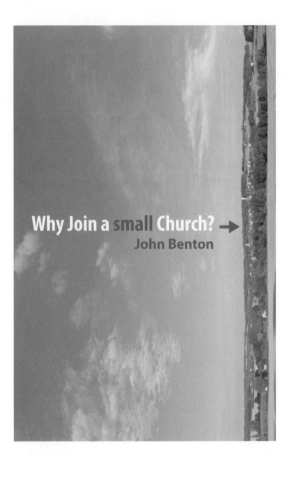

Why Join a small Church?
John Benton

Why Join a small Church?
by John Benton

"A Christian married couple I know of had to move out of London and leave their church to go north with the husband's job."

"Much to the surprise of some of their long-term Christian pals they began attending the little and very local Anglican church in the village to which they had moved. The Christian friends of the couple had concerns. The church was small, the teaching was not heretical but it was not great, and there was nothing there for their four children.

"It was while talking through these concerns one evening with one of their friends that the husband made a comment which was highly significant. He said, 'How could we drive past one church to go to another?' They felt, before God, they just could not do it.

"They refused to dismiss the little church because it was in a poorly state. They were more concerned to help Christ's cause there than they were for their own immediate welfare or 'enjoyment' of the ministry.

"To join a big and thriving church is not always wrong, but it is frequently the easy option. To join a little, needy congregation is not a decision to be taken lightly. It will probably require far more guts, love, resilience and spiritual exertion. But how the devil would love to herd Christians into a few big city centre churches, getting them to travel miles from their communities, and leaving vast tracts of our country with no viable witness for the gospel.

"This book is written as a plea for Christians to think again about getting involved with a small church. Ask yourself the question, 'How can we drive past one church to go to another?'"

ISBN: 978-1-84550-407-6

Christian Focus Publications

Our mission statement –

STAYING FAITHFUL

In dependence upon God we seek to impact the world through literature faithful to His infallible Word, the Bible. Our aim is to ensure that the Lord Jesus Christ is presented as the only hope to obtain forgiveness of sin, live a useful life and look forward to heaven with Him.

Our books are published in four imprints:

CHRISTIAN FOCUS

Popular works including biographies, commentaries, basic doctrine and Christian living.

CHRISTIAN HERITAGE

Books representing some of the best material from the rich heritage of the church.

MENTOR

Books written at a level suitable for Bible College and seminary students, pastors, and other serious readers. The imprint includes commentaries, doctrinal studies, examination of current issues and church history.

CF4·K

Children's books for quality Bible teaching and for all age groups: Sunday school curriculum, puzzle and activity books; personal and family devotional titles, biographies and inspirational stories – because you are never too young to know Jesus!

Christian Focus Publications Ltd,
Geanies House, Fearn, Ross-shire,
IV20 1TW, Scotland, United Kingdom.
www.christianfocus.com
blog.christianfocus.com